SACRED TEXTS

THE
GNOSTIC
GOSPELS

Including
The Gospel of Thomas
The Gospel of Mary Magdalene

Alan Jacobs

Introduction by
Revd Dr Vrej N. Nersessian

WATKINS
LONDON

This edition produced in 2005 for Sacred Texts,
an imprint of Watkins Publishing,
Sixth Floor, Castle House, 75–76 Wells Street,
London W1T 3QH

1 3 5 7 9 10 8 6 4 2

ISBN 1 84293 099 0

Typeset in Great Britain by Jerry Goldie Graphic Design
Printed and bound in Thailand by Imago

British Library Cataloguing in Publication data available

www.watkinspublishing.com

CONTENTS

FOREWORD

As discovered at Nag Hammadi, the Gnostic Gospels,
written mainly in Early Coptic, are severely fragmented and
full of lacunas. My aim has been to provide a clear, readable
text that preserves the essential meaning, hence obscurities
and needless repetitions have been omitted from some tracts.

From the fifty-three texts discovered, I have chosen the
thirteen reproduced here because I felt they were potentially
of greater interest to the contemporary reader. In addition,
unlike some of the remaining texts, they are not abounding
in archaisms and strangely coined proper names whose
derivation and usage have largely been lost.

The selected Gospels reveal sayings of Christ not
included in the New Testament and throw light on the
intimate relationship between Jesus and his disciples. The
Gospel of Mary Magdalene, for example, gives details of his
relationship with this favoured disciple. Other texts show
the structure of Gnostic cosmology.

My poetic transcription is in free verse form, paraphrased
from the widely differing literal prose translations in
existence. I have relied on my own practical knowledge of
the mystical path in the higher religious traditions to make
as much sense as possible of these truly beautiful, ecstatic
and awe-inspiring texts.

Alan Jacobs

INTRODUCTION

Jewish beliefs marked Christianity permanently until the fourth century, when Jewish Christians who had been prominent in the New Testament were reduced to a remnant. Those who survived had their own *"Gospel according to the Hebrews"*. They denied the Virgin birth of Jesus, but others accepted it while denying that he had existed before his adoption by the Holy Spirit. These believers were called Ebionites, meaning "poor". Eusebius believed that the term was appropriate because of their "poor and low opinions of Christ". Origin, a prolific author of the early Church, quoted an Ebionite belief that Jesus had said he had been "taken by my mother the Holy Spirit by one of the hairs of my head". Another poetic expression ridiculed by Christian literature was a version of the Trinity where the Son is described as "the cup", the Father as "he who was milked", and the Spirit as "She who milked him". This comes from The Odes of Solomon, a collection of hymns found in 1905. One hymn says about Jesus:

> His love for me brought low his greatness …
> He took my nature so that I might understand him,
> My face so that I should not turn away from him.

The last among these hymns portrays Jesus as "the Just One hanged by the roadside", moving from his cross to join the dead and saying:

They ran towards me, the dead ...
And I heard their voices and
wrote my name on their heads,
So they are free and they are mine,
Alleluia!

Christian teaching had become hostile to Judaism, as
evidenced in the Letter of Barnabas, written in the second
century. It was claimed that an evil spirit had inspired the
Jews to misunderstand the purposes of God throughout their
history. Ignatius, in the second century, did not hesitate to talk
about Jesus as "our God", whatever might be the objections
of Jews. In his Letter to the Magnesians he wrote, "God is one
and has revealed himself to his Son Jesus Christ, who is his
Word issuing from silence." But he said that the zeal of the
Christians in Ephesus had been aroused by "God's blood" and
begged the Christians in Rome not to try to prevent his own
martyrdom: "Let me imitate the suffering of my God." He was
not interested in offering any philosophical defence of such
expressions, for the main thrust of his message was a plea for
Christians to unite; he was less interested in finding common
ground with Jews or with any others who did not share his
faith. His life's ambition was "to become God's wheat, and I
am ground by the teeth of wild beasts so that I may become
Christ's pure loaf ... Come fire, cross, a battle with wild beasts,
the wrenching of bones, the mangling of limbs, the crushing
of my whole body, the cruel tortures of the Devil – only let
me get to Jesus Christ." He also said, "my Love is crucified",
meaning that his own human passions had died with Jesus.
Paul had expressed a similar sentiment, but Ignatius went

beyond the more balanced Paul by saying plainly that he was "in love with death". The Armenian poet Gregory of Narek (951–1003) likens his relationship to Christ to "the wick in the candle":

> You gave the oil, and in this oil you placed a wick
> which exemplifies your union, without imperfection,
> with our condition, formed and woven with
> your love of mankind.
> [Gregory of Narek, *Book of Lamentations,* Erevan, 1985]

Christianity's main partners in the fourth century were not Jews but pagans, or, more often, people who were seeking reality in religion and not finding it in either Judaism or paganism. The great question was, What did such seekers have to believe in order to be Christians? If Christianity was no longer a Jewish sect, how far could it go as it left its Palestinian birthplace? Could it go on to speak about mysteries hitherto left to what Ignatius had called "the silence"?

Answers were given by a number of movements lumped together under the name "Gnostics", derived from the Greek word *gnosis*, first mentioned in 1 Timothy 6.20. This name was used to cover groups of people who were not content with the statements of faith and modes of behaviour that had been handed down and widely accepted. The principal character-istic of Gnosticism in its many shapes and forms was a negative evaluation of the material world and, therefore, of its Creator. Dualistic language about spirit and matter, usually cast in mythological form, was common, and the distinctiveness of different sects often lay in the imaginative myths by which individual teachers expressed their dualism. They speculated about the origins of the cosmos and how the human soul came to be imprisoned in a body of flesh. The theme from The Gospel of St John – that the divine Logos had united human flesh to himself – was difficult to grasp for anyone who thought the flesh vile. It seemed altogether easier to think of the divine Logos being united to the human soul and not to the human body.

At the time when Gnostic movements were shaping their mythologies there was no fixed canon of the New Testament writings, and Gnostic teachers were proud to be able to produce *Secret Saying of Jesus*, accounts of what Jesus had said to his disciples between the Resurrection and the Ascension. The Gospels, Acts, Letters and Apocalypses widely current were not limited to those which in the course of time became the New Testament. There were also Gnostic texts which "the Church" did not recognise as authoritative and which were excluded from the canon.

In 1945, in a village in Upper Egypt called Nag Hammadi, a camel driver uncovered a jar containing the remains of thirteen codices. Analysis of the materials used in the bindings of the codices shows that they had been produced in the area in which they were found. Dates on letters and grain receipts indicate a date in the mid fourth century AD. References to the Coptic monk Pachom were proof that the volumes had been in the possession of the Pachomian monks who inhabited the area.

The works in the collection may have been a library in use by Gnostics, or they may have been copied by monks in Upper Egypt who were intending to refute Gnostic claims. Or, because orthodoxy and heresy were so intermingled among ascetics in that region, they may have served to defend the practices of the monks, while the more heretical works were later separated and entombed, when, in 367, Athanasius sent out a letter condemning apocryphal books.

The writings in the collection were translated into Coptic from Greek. A few that provided striking examples of the teaching of the Gnostics were published within a decade and became well known: The Gospel of Truth, The Treatise on Resurrection, The Gospel of Thomas, The Gospel of Philip, The Apocryphon of John, The Wisdom of Jesus. These writings represent an ascetic position with regard to the material world and its passions. One of the most striking features of the teaching is the elaborate mythology that explains how this world of darkness, dominated by a demonic god and his powers, came into being. Most of these myths begin with a harmonious unfolding of the heavenly world from an indescribable divinity. The divinity may be represented as a "one" beyond all beings or may be given the epithet "Mother–Father". Since matter, passions, darkness and discord have nothing in common with the divine, the myths eventually tell the story of a "fall" or a "flaw" in the heavenly realm. Often, this "flaw" is the restless desire of the youngest of the divine beings, Wisdom *(Pistis Sophia*, British Library, Add. 5114). She may be seeking the divine Father above or she may try to give birth without her heavenly consort, as the mother–father does.

Alan Jacobs, a poet relying on his personal and practical knowledge of the mystical path in religion, has selected extracts from fifty-three Gnostic texts that shed light on these esoteric doctrines. His inspired poetic translations give us a glimpse of the more attractive side of Gnosticism. Whatever else Jesus Christ might have been, the Church refused to make him a demigod, and the various forms of speculation that were defined as Gnostic coined terms and conceptions which did attempt to bridge the gulf. The most popular Gospel is that of Thomas, sometimes called the "fifth Gospel" for its very close resemblance to the canonical Gospels. It contains 114 "sayings" of Jesus [*logia*], introduced by the simple formula "Jesus said", including the parable of the sower, the grain of mustard seed, the tares, the pearl of great price, the leaven, the lost sheep, the treasure hidden in a field. But the Coptic text almost never corresponds word for word with that of the canonical Gospels. The centre of interest is *gnosis,* a profound knowledge that depends on the interpretation of the secret words *(logion 1)*, and begins with knowledge of oneself *(logion 3)*. The person of the Revealer is himself a mystery. To know him will make Thomas the equal of Jesus *(logion 13)*. It is this *gnosis* that Jesus brings, "that which the eye has not seen, and the ear has not heard" *(logion 17)*. The disciples already possess the beginning of the truth *(logion 18)*, but they will have to "work" in order that *gnosis* may produce its fruits in them *(logion 20)*. They will be watchful with regard to the evil powers, those "robbers" who threaten them *(logion 21)*. Let there be among them "a man forwarned", that is to say, a Gnostic sage.

Gnostic authors speak of God in imagery that is both male and female. "I am the Father; I am the Mother; I am the Son," God says in The Apocryphon of John. Elsewhere a spirit of wisdom announces, "I am the Voice ... in the likeness of a female ... in the thought of the likeness of my masculinity ...

I am androgynous ..." The unification of the sexes served in early Christianity as a symbol of salvation, and in the memorable announcement of St Paul in his Letter to the Galatians, in Christ "there is neither male nor female; for you are all one in Christ" (Gal. 3:28). Paul borrows this text from Gnostic literature. The theme of "making the male and female into a single one" is also explicit in The Gospel of Thomas. And in The Gospel of Mary Magdalene the apostle Levi admonishes Peter "for doubting a woman as worthy", reminding Peter that:

> If Jesus made her upright,
> who are we to disown her?
> Jesus knew her well, that's
> why he loved her more than us.
> Let's be penitent ...

Also shared by Gnosticism and Orthodox writers was a sense that Christ was really polymorphous, that he had many different appearances depending on who was perceiving him. The chameleon-like changeability of Christ in early Christian art may be linked to the belief that the Lord "hath no form nor comeliness" (Isaiah 53: 2).

Christianity, having opted for the most "visual", "tangible" and "materialist" expressions, has deprived its followers of the need to "seek", to "search", to "look for the 'hidden'". The formulaic definition of the "mystery profound" within fixed doctrines has meant that these positions outside their historical context have become incomprehensible, irrelevant and absurd. Today, Christianity constantly needs to re-invent itself.

The twelfth-century Armenian poet Nerses Shnorhali

(1102–73) teaches that man, in spite of his fallen state, is still in "the image of God, and paradise is his habitation". Claiming a secret divine wisdom specially revealed to the initiates – "to be the Revealer of the hidden treasures" – humans ascend to the spiritual and to the rational enjoyment of the good tidings of God, which the eye has not seen, the ear has not heard, which the heart of man has not recalled, and which God has prepared for his loved ones.

For the modern reader, Alan Jacobs' inspired poetic translation has captured the awesome beauty of the original Gospels, "to make us finders of the hidden treasures":

> His disciples asked,
> "On which day will you
> make yourself known to us?"
> Lord Jesus replied,
> "When you rid yourselves
> of guilt and shame."

Alan Jacobs' skill in his craft has freed Gnostic texts of their tedious and grotesque theosophical speculations to reveal a completely different aspect – mystical, devotional, poetical.

Revd Dr Vrej N. Nersessian
Curator, The British Library
Christian Middle East Section

THE FABLE OF
THE PEARL

A dramatic Greek myth depicting the
Soul's bodily incarnation and its eventual liberation.
Attributed to Jude Thomas the Apostle, it summarises the
"Gnostic Call" to awaken from the dream of life into Self or
God Realisation.

FROM *The Apocryphal Acts of the Apostle Thomas*

When I was an innocent child
I lived in my father's house,
enjoying the love of all
who reared me.

Then my parents sent me
from our Eastern home,
with enough goods for a long trip.

They burdened me
with treasure light
enough to bear alone:

gold from ancient hills,
silver plate and goblets,
emeralds from India and
agates from Kosa, but they
stripped me of my robe of glory.

This they'd woven
from generous love,
with a jewel-studded
purple cloak that fitted well.

They drew up a deed,
impressing it on my heart
and memory.

"Go down to Egypt, fetch that
one pearl from the ocean bed,
kept by a fierce serpent.
Then you can wear your robe again,
your precious cloak, and with
your brother inherit our kingdom."

I left with two friends,
for the path was dangerous
and I was young.

I passed through Maishan,
and their greedy merchants,
then came to Babel,
and entered seedy Sarburg.
I'd arrived in Egypt.

My friends left.
I went close to the serpent;
I stayed at an inn until
he fell asleep and I could
seize the pearl.

Since I was One
and stayed with my Self
I was unrecognised by
my fellow guests.

But I saw one youth
like myself, a son of the King,
an initiated one.

He introduced himself
and became my friend,
someone in whom I could confide.

He warned me about the Egyptians,
and making friends with the impure.

But I had to wear clothes like theirs
or they might suspect I was a stranger
who planned to steal the pearl.

Yet they suspected
I wasn't one of them,
and slyly bedevilled me,
giving me strong drink
and spiced meats.

I soon forgot I was the King's son
and slaved for their Pharoah.

I even forgot the pearl.
After their heavy food and
rich drink I fell into a deep sleep.

My parents heard about all
that happened and were very sad.

It was announced in our kingdom
that all must return.

The Kings of Parthia
and Eastern nobles
decided I mustn't stay in Egypt.

They sent me a letter,
"From your father
the King of Kings.
Your mother, the Eastern Queen,
your brother, next in line,
all send greetings.

Awake from sleep!
Remember you're the son
of a Great King,
see to whom you're enslaved!

Recall the precious pearl
and why you left for Egypt,
and your robe of glory
and your purple cloak,
so you can wear them again
and your name be written
in the Hero's Book,
and with your brother
succeed to our kingdom."

This letter from the King
was sealed by his right hand
and contained a message
warning against the evil folk
of Babel and Sarburg.

It flew before me
carried by an eagle,
king of the birds.
It landed beside me
and the bird began to sing!

The golden tone of his
song woke me up!
I held and stroked him,
broke the seal, and read.

Then I remembered
I was the son of a Great King
and that my pure soul
yearned and craved
for its own likeness.

I recalled the priceless pearl
for which I had gone down
into the land of Egypt.

I went to the serpent
and charmed him to sleep,
constantly repeating,
again and again, my father's name,
and that of my brother, next in line,
and my mother, Queen of the East.

I seized the precious pearl
and fled quickly, to return
to my beloved father.

I threw off my filthy
Egyptian smock,
leaving it behind.
Recollecting my Self
I went east to come home.

This clarion letter lit my path,
and by its clarity encouraged me,
and by its love, led me on.

I remembered my robe and
purple cloak, which I had
left in my parents' house, and
the treasures they'd given me.
When I pictured the robe in its
full glory it suddenly seemed to be
a reflection of my Real Self.

I saw my own Self in this clear mirror,
knowing the see-er and the seen
were not two but One.

The King of Kings was imaged there
shimmering all over, as the true Gnosis.

I saw He was poised to sing,
and I heard the murmur of His song.

"I Am That Power, which
acted in the acts of he who was
reared in his father's house."

I noted my strength grew
according to my efforts.

With kingly grace
He poured love on me,
with heraldic hands
hastening me to drink.

My love raced to greet Him,
I expanded, cladding myself
with His rainbow hues.
I threw His royal cloak
over my whole Self.

Well robed I entered
the pearly gate of prostration
and adoration.

I bowed my head,
kneeled and worshiped
in my Father's Presence.
His will I obeyed,
in response to the
fulfilment of His promise.

He received me with
open arms and holy joy.
I was with Him in His kingdom.

The seraphim praised
Him with loud song.

"Hallelujah! Holy, holy,
holy is the Lord of Hosts,
the whole Earth is full
of His glory."

He had honoured His
covenant, that I would
come to His Court,
The King of Kings.

For I had found the pearl
beyond price and would be
with Him Eternally.

THE GOSPEL OF THOMAS

A primary scripture of the Early Eastern
Church, recorded by Jude Thomas the Apostle, relating
intimate Gnostic sayings of Jesus to his disciples, many of
which do not appear in the New Testament. Originally
written in Greek before AD 200.

These are the secret words
of Almighty God,
which Lord Jesus Christ
uttered and were scribed by
his disciple Thomas.

He said, "He who comprehends
the inner meaning of these words
will be immortal.

Permit whoever seeks
never to cease from seeking
until he finds.

When he succeeds
he will be turned around;
when he's so turned
he'll be amazed and shall
rule over the All.

If those who lead you
say 'God's Kingdom's in Heaven,'
then birds will fly there first.
If they say 'It's in the sea,'
the fish will swim there first.

For God's Kingdom dwells in
your heart and all around you;
when you know your Self
you too shall be known!

You'll be aware that you're
the sons and daughters of
our living Father.

But if you fail to know
your own Self
you're in hardship
and are that hardship."

His disciples enquired,
"Should we fast?
How should we pray?
Should we give to charity?
What should we eat?"

Lord Jesus replied,
"Don't lie!
Don't do what you hate!
All's seen by Heaven.
There's nothing hidden
that won't be made known.
There's nothing secret
that will stay concealed
without first being shown.

Happy is the lion
that a man will eat;
the lion will become a man.
Cursed is the man whom
the lion eats for that lion
will become a man.

Man is like a skilled
angler who casts his net

and draws it up, full of fish.
Among them he finds
big and small fish.
He throws back the small
and keeps the large.

He who has his ears wide open,
let him hear!

A sower went to sow.
He filled his hand with seeds
and scattered them on the field.

Some fell on the path,
rooks flew down and ate them;
some fell on rocks and failed to root.

Others fell on thorns that choked
them, and worms ate them up.
Some fell on good soil
and grew good fruit,
sixty times the measure
and even double.

I've set fire to this world,
to keep it blazing until
it burns away.
Heaven will pass away;
that which is above heaven
will also pass away.

Dead souls don't live,
live souls don't die;
yet when you treat dead souls
you bring them alive.

When you're in the Light
what will you do?
At birth you were One,
then you made two.
What will you do?"

The disciples asked,
"We know you'll leave us.
Who'll then rule over us?"

Jesus replied,
"Wherever you arrive,
go to James who is righteous,

because of whom, even heaven
and earth came into existence;
now tell me whom I resemble."

Simon Peter answered him first,
"You're like a righteous angel."
Matthew said, "You're like
A sage or lover of wisdom."
Thomas said, "My lips won't let
me say you're like anyone."

Jesus replied,
"I'm no longer your Master
because you've drunk
from living water.
You're enlivened
by the bubbling source
which I've caused to flow."

He took Thomas on one side
and addressed three sayings
of Almighty God to him.
When Thomas returned
they enquired, "What did
Jesus say?"

Thomas replied,
"If I tell you what he said
you'll pick up stones
and hurl them at me;
fire will rise up from them
and burn you all up!"

Lord Jesus then said,
"If you fast you'll get into sin;
if you pray for boons
you'll be condemned;
when you give alms
you may wound your spirit.

When you go to other lands,
into their countryside,
if they welcome you,
eat what they provide
and heal their sick.
What enters your sight won't
harm you, but what comes out
of your mouth can defile you.

When you see He who's
unborn from a womb,

prostrate and worship,
for He's your Father.

Men believe I've come to
bring peace to this world,
but they don't understand
that I've come to bring
divisions on earth,
fire, struggle and strife.

If there are five in a house,
three will fight two,
two will fight three.
Father versus son,
son against father;
they'll stand up better
being alone.

I'll show you what
no eye has seen,
no ear has heard,
no hand has touched,
and what is not yet risen
in men's hearts."

The disciples then said,
"Tell us what our end will be."

He answered,
"Have you seen the beginning
that you may know the end?
Where there's a beginning
there's no end.
Happy is the man or woman
who can stand bravely
at the beginning.
He or she shall know the
end and won't taste death."

The disciples then enquired
about the Kingdom of Heaven.

Jesus replied, "It's like a
grain of mustard, smaller than
other seeds, but when it falls
on ploughed ground it grows
a large stem and shelters the birds."

Mary asked Lord Jesus,
"Whom are your disciples like?"

He replied, "Like small children
living in a field which isn't theirs.

When the owners return
they'll demand their land back;
the disciples have to strip off
their outer pretensions
and pay back their loan.

So if the landlord of the house
knows a burglar is coming
he'll stay awake before he breaks in.
He'll not allow the rogue
to steal his goods.

So, watch this world;
get ready for deeds
with great strength,
otherwise thieves will
find a way to break into you,
and the reward you expect,
they'll get.

In your heart let there be
a man of understanding!

When the corn ripens
he comes in haste,
sickle in hand, and reaps!
He who has his ears wide open,
let him hear!"

Lord Jesus saw babies
being breast fed.
He said to his disciples,
"These infants being suckled
are like those who enter
my Father's House."

They answered,
"Shall we, being as children,
come into His Kingdom?"

Jesus replied,
"Make the two into One
and the inner as the outer
and the outer as the inner,
the above as below,
the male and female
into a single One.

So the male isn't male and
the female isn't female any more.
When you make two eyes
into a single eye,
a hand into a hand,
a foot into a foot,
a picture into a picture,
then you'll enter the Kingdom.

I'll choose you,
as one from a thousand;
you'll stand bravely,
being a single One."

His disciples said, "Show us
that place where you are;
we need to search for it."

He answered, "If you have ears
then pay attention and listen!

There's perfect Light
at the heart of a Man of Light;
he lights up the whole world.
If he fails to shine there's darkness.

If you don't give up the world
you won't find the Kingdom.
If you don't keep the Sabbath
as a real Sabbath,
you won't know my Father.

I stood bravely
in the middle of the world;
I came in a body.
I found them drunk!
None were thirsty.

My soul was afflicted for
mankind, for they are blind
at heart and do not see.
Empty, they enter this world,
empty they'll leave!

But now they're drunk!
When they sober up they'll
change their Knowledge.

A fortified city built on a
high mountain will not fall,
nor is it a secret.

What you hear clearly
between your two ears,
shout from the roof tops.
Nobody lights a lamp and
hides it; instead they put it
on a stand so everyone can
enjoy its light.

If a blind man guides the blind,
they'll both slip into a ditch.
It's impossible to enter
the house of a strong man
and win it by force.
One must bind his hands,
then one can enter.

Have no cares from dawn
until night for what you try."

His disciples asked,
"On which day will you
make yourself known to us?"

Lord Jesus replied,
"When you rid yourselves

of guilt and shame and tear off
your old rags and trample them
beneath your feet like children.

Then you'll see the Son of
He who is the living God,
and you'll never need fear again.

Many years you've yearned to hear
these words of God which I give you.
You've no one else
from whom to hear them;
there'll be days when you
look for me and fail to find me.

To he who holds the Truth
in his hand, more shall be handed;
he who doesn't hold the Truth,
even the little he has shall be taken away.
Be your Self, especially when
you're approaching death."

His disciples enquired,
"Who are you that you can say
these words to us?"

Lord Jesus answered,
"From what I say
can't you see who I am?
But you're like those Jews
who love the tree and shun its fruit,
or love the fruit and shun the tree.

He who blasphemes against
my father shall be forgiven,
but he who blasphemes
against the holy Spirit
shall not be forgiven,
in earth or in heaven.

Grapes aren't picked
from thorn bushes,
nor are figs found on thistles.

A good man brings
virtue out of his barn;
a bad man brings ill will
from the evil stored in his heart.
He spreads guile from his heart's
plenty and spreads wickedness.

From Adam until John the Baptist,
among children of the womb
there's none higher than he.

John has a vision
that won't be blurred.
But as I've said, he among you
who becomes like a small child
shall know the kingdom
and be greater than John.

If two make peace in their one house,
they'll say with faith to the mountain
'Move!' and it will move.

Happy are the solitary
and those chosen, for they
shall find God's Kingdom.
If you seek it in your heart
you shall enter again."

His disciples asked,
"On which day will peace
for the dead come about?
When will a new world come?"

Jesus replied,
"What you desire
has already come,
but you don't realise it."

His disciples said,
"Two dozen prophets
spoke to Israel;
they all prophesied
your true nature."

Jesus replied,
"You've ignored
he who lives with you,
and you've spoken
about the dead.

He who knows this world
has found a corpse;
he who has found a corpse,
this world finds unworthy.

The Kingdom of heaven is like
a farmer who bought good seed;

his foe came one night, stole his
seeds and then sowed weeds.

The farmer forbade his
workmen to hoe the weeds,
saying, 'In pulling the weeds
you may ruin the wheat too.'

But I say, at harvest time
the weeds will crop;
they must all be hoed
and burnt!"

Jesus and his disciples
saw a Samaritan
travelling to Judea
carrying a lamb.

Jesus said, "Why does
he bear that lamb?"

They answered,
"To kill and eat it.
While it's alive he can't eat it,
only when it's dead can he dine."

Jesus then said,
"You yourselves, find the
place of peace within,
or you too will be like
dead lambs and be eaten!

I tell my cryptic parables
to those worthy to hear them.
Whatever effort your right side
may attempt, don't let your left
know what it tries.

There was a rich man who
said, 'I'll use my wealth
to sow, reap and plant
and fill up my barns
so I lack nothing.'
That night he died.

He who has ears wide open,
let him hear!

A man planned a feast;
when he'd prepared the food
he sent his servant to invite the guests.

The servant met the first
and said, 'My master
asks you to dinner.'

The man answered,
'I've got money ready
for some merchants;
they'll come this evening,
and I wish to place some orders,
so I'm sorry, I can't come.'

He went to another and said,
'My master invites you to dinner.'
The man answered,
'I've just bought a farm.
I must collect the rents,
so I'm sorry, I can't come.'

The servant went back and
told his master that those
he'd invited couldn't come.

The master told his servant,
'Go out on the street and
bring any you can find
so they may come and eat.'

So you see, busy business people
will not enter the house of my Father.

Show me the stone
that the builders have rejected;
that one shall be my corner stone.

He who understands all
but lacks Self Knowledge lacks all.

Be happy when you're
reviled and harassed;
but peace won't be found
if your mind harasses you at heart."

A man said to Jesus,
"Please tell my brothers to share
my father's goods with me."

Jesus answered,
"Oh man, who made me to be
a divider; is that who I am?

The harvest is great,
the labourers are few and sluggish;

pray to the Lord to send good workmen.
There are many looking down the well,
but few are diving deeply.

I am the Light above them all;
I am the All; the All issues from me
and reaches me.

Cut wood, I am there;
lift stone, I am there.

Why did you come here
to my countryside?
To see a reed shaken by the wind,
or a man clothed in soft garments?

Your kings and nobles wear fine
robes but do not know Truth!"

A woman from the mob
that had gathered said,
"Blessed is the womb
that gave birth to you,
my Lord, and the breasts
that suckled you."

He answered,
"Happy are all those
who've heard my words,
the hidden secrets of my
Father, The Living God, and
have kept them in good Faith.

For there may come a
time when you'll say,
'Happy is the womb
that didn't give birth,
and the breasts that didn't feed.'

He that loves the world,
identifies with his body,
and he who does so,
the world is unworthy of him.

He who's become rich,
let him be king,
and he who has power,
let him abandon it.

He who is near to me
is close to the fire,

and he who is distant
is far from my Kingdom.

Pictures are seen by men,
but that pure Light which
reveals them lies veiled.

In the reflection
of my Father's Light
His Light will be seen;
but His image will be
hidden by His Light.

On the day you see the
Light of your own true Self,
you'll rejoice!

But if you only see forms
which from the beginning
were in you, and don't die
to them or know them,
how can you stand the Light?

Adam was created from a vast
power and great fecundity.

He wasn't fit for you
for had he been worthy
he wouldn't have known
spiritual death.

Foxes have holes,
birds boast nests;
the Son of Man has
no den where he can
lay down his head and rest.

Decadent is the soul
that depends on the body;
miserable is the man
attached to the flesh.

Angels and Prophets will
visit you and hand you
what is truly yours.
You must give back
what's in your keeping.

Pray to your Self and ask,
'When will they come
to collect what's theirs?'

Why do you clean only
the lip of a cup when
He who made the inner
also made the outer?

Follow me!
My yoke is easy,
my lordship is gentle;
you'll find peace."

The disciples asked,
"Who are you?
So that we may trust you."

Lord Jesus replied,
"You merely contemplate
the surface of heaven and earth,
but he who stands before you
you don't know; nor do you
know how to find out.

Search and you shall find!
But what you've asked me
I held from telling you;
now I wish to speak.

But you do not seek
after Self Knowledge.

Don't waste good food on dogs;
they leave it on a dung heap.

Don't hand pearls to pigs;
they'll pollute them.

He who earnestly and
persistently seeks, shall find!
To him who knocks hard,
the door will be opened.

If you have money,
don't lend just for interest,
but give it to him who needs it.

The Kingdom of Heaven
is like a good woman who
takes leaven, hides it in dough
and bakes loaves.

Those that have ears to hear,
let them hear!

The Kingdom of Heaven is
also like a foolish woman carrying
a load of flour on a long road;
the sack splits and flour pours out,
but she doesn't realise.
Because she doesn't see what
has happened, she isn't worried,
but she gets home her sack is empty.

The Kingdom of Heaven
is like a brave soldier
wishing to slay a giant;
he draws his sword at home
and strikes through the wall
to test his confidence.
Then he goes and kills the giant."

His disciples said,
"Your mother and brothers
are waiting outside."
He replied, "All those here
who do the will of my Father
are my mother and brothers;
they're the ones who will enter
the Kingdom of Heaven."

The disciples showed Jesus
a gold shekel, saying,
"Caesar's collectors
demand taxes from us."
Jesus replied, "Hand to
Caesar what is Caesar's,
to God what is God's,
and what is mine hand to me.

He who doesn't reject
his mother and father
because of my teaching
won't become my disciple,
for my mother gave me birth
but my real Mother gave me life.

Pity the Pharisees;
they're like dogs
sleeping in an ox's shed.
They neither eat nor
let the ox eat.

Blessed is the man who
knows when thieves will
break into his house.

He can get up, collect himself, and
be ready to act before they come."

The disciples said,
"Let's pray and fast today."
Jesus answered, "What sin
have I committed or by what
have I been conquered?
When the bridegroom leaves
the bridal chamber, then
we'll fast and pray.

He who knows his real
Mother and Father, can he
be called the son of a whore?
When you make two into
One you'll be sons of Man,
and if you command a
mountain to move, it will move.

The Kingdom of Heaven
is like the good shepherd
who owned a hundred sheep.
When the fattest was lost he
left all the others until he found it.

He told his flock, 'I loved that one
more than the rest.'

He who drinks my words with
understanding shall be like me,
and I shall become him and the
secret things will be revealed.

The Kingdom of Heaven
is like the farmer who owned
a field with buried treasure
that he did not know was there.

When he died he left the land
to his son, who, also being
ignorant, sold the field.

The man who bought it found
the gold while ploughing and
was able to grant loans at a
fair rate of interest.

He who has known this
world and become wealthy,
let him disown it.

The earth and heavens
may turn back before you,
but he who is truly alive
won't know fear or death.

He who finds himself
to be of this world is unfit.

Pity the body that
leans upon the soul;
pity the soul that
leans upon the flesh."

His disciples enquired,
"On what day will
the Kingdom come?"

Lord Jesus replied, "It won't
come through anticipation;
they won't say, 'Look, it's here,
or look over there.'

The Kingdom of Heaven
covers the Earth with glory,
but mankind fails to see it!"

Simon Peter said to the
Lord and his disciples,
"Let Mary leave us, because women
are unfit for the Life Everlasting."

Jesus replied,
"Wait, I'll guide her soul,
to make her as a real man,
in that place which transcends
the differences between the sexes,
so she'll become a living spirit.

For each woman who makes
herself male in this way
and overcomes all differences
will enter the Kingdom of Heaven!"

THE GOSPEL OF
MARY MAGDALENE

Originally written in Greek, the Gospel of
Mary Magdalene tells the disciples about Mary's unique
revelations through her relationship with Jesus.
Andrew and Peter question her veracity and ask why a
woman should become a favourite disciple.
They are admonished by Levi.

Mary questioned her Master,
"At the end of an aeon,
will all matter be destroyed?"

Jesus answered,
"All of nature, its forms and
creatures are interrelated;
all will be returned to their
original source.

The essence of matter also returns
to the source of its own nature.
He who has ears, let him comprehend!"

Peter said, "As you've told us
almost everything, tell us this also:
what is the world's sin?"

Jesus replied,
"There is no sin in reality!
It is you who create sin,
when you do deeds, such as adultery,
that are called sinful.

That's why Good enters your heart
to return you back to your source.

This is why you get ill
and eventually die;
he who understands,
let him understand.

Matter caused powerful passions
to enter into you, forces which
come from its opposites in nature.

Then a sickness arises in the body;
so be of strong faith!
If you're weak, gather strength

in the presence of Nature;
he who has ears to hear,
let him hear!"

Then Jesus greeted them saying,
"Peace be with you all.
Take my peace into your Selves;
be watchful so nobody leads
you astray claiming 'Look there,
look here for the son of man.'

I tell you that the son of man
is within you all!
Seek him inside; those who
search diligently and earnestly
shall surely find him.

Then leave and preach the truth
of the Kingdom to those with
ears to hear; don't invent rules
beyond those I've given.

Don't make laws like law-makers do
or else you'll be held back."
After he had said this he left.

The disciples were upset.
They complained,
"How can we go to the Gentiles
and preach the truth of the
Kingdom of the Son of Man?
If they won't save him,
how will they save us?"

The Mary rose and said,
"Don't grieve! Be brave;
his grace is always with you
to guard you.

Let's praise his magnitude;
he's prepared us and turned us
into real men and women!"

When Mary said this
she lifted their hearts up to the Good;
they started to study his words.

Peter said to Mary, "Dear sister,
we know our Saviour loves
you more than the rest of women.

Tell us his words that you remember,
those we've never heard before."

Mary answered,
"What's concealed from you I'll tell;
I saw him in a vision and I told him.

He said, 'Blessed are you that
your strength wasn't shaken by
my appearance, for where the
heart is lies buried treasure.'

I asked, 'Lord, does he or she
who sees the vision perceive
it through soul or spirit?'

He answered, 'One perceives
through neither soul nor spirit
but by mind, which mediates
between both; visions are mental.'

I pondered. 'I never saw you descend,
now I see you ascend.
Why does my mind deceive me
since you are part of me?'

My soul answered,
'But you didn't recognise me;
I serve you as your robe
but you don't know me.'
When the voice ended
I rejoiced inwardly.

When I came to ponder on ignorance,
the third dark power,
it questioned my soul saying,
'Where are you heading?
You're enslaved by evil,
so don't judge me.'

My soul replied,
'Why judge me; I haven't
judged you. I was imprisoned,
although I never imprisoned.
I wasn't recognised, but I've known
that All is being destroyed,
both in earth and heaven.'

When my soul had conquered ignorance
it rose up and saw the fourth power,
which assumes seven forms.

The first is darkness, the second
desire, then ignorance, fear of death,
power of the flesh, foolish reason,
and self-righteous pedantry.

These are the powers of anger
and doubt; they ask, 'From where
did you come, killer of men;
where are you heading,
slayer of space?'

My soul replied,
'What bound me is dead,
what enveloped me has been
vanquished; my desires are over
and ignorance is no more.

In this life I was freed from the
world and the chains of forgetfulness.
From now on I will rest
in the eternal now; for this age,
this aeon, and in stillness.'"

Then Mary was silent, for this was
the truth Jesus had revealed.

Andrew then spoke,
"Say what you like about
what Mary has said, but I
don't believe Jesus would tell
us such strange notions!"

Peter said, "Did he really speak
with Mary, a woman, without our
knowing? Are we to listen to her?
Did he favour her more than us?"

Then Mary cried to Peter,
"My brother, do you believe
I made this up, or that I would
lie about Jesus?"

Levi admonished Peter,
"You've always been
quick to anger;
now I see you doubting
a woman as worthy as Mary.

Who do you think you are
to dispute her testimony,
like an enemy?

If Jesus made her upright,
who are we to disown her?
Jesus knew her well; that's
why he loved her more than us.

Let's be penitent and don the robe
of the perfect man and make him
one with ourselves, as he taught.

Let's proclaim his word,
not make more laws beyond
those he ordered!"

The disciples then disbanded
and began to teach his Gospel.

MELCHIZEDEK

An Apocalyptic Gospel, originally written in Greek,
telling of the visions received from celestial beings by the
legendary Melchizedek. It contains prophecies concerning
the death, ministry and resurrection of Jesus and the
heretics who will deny him.

"I speak about Jesus, Son of God,
who came from the Aeon that speaks
about all Aeons and their nature;
so I may be fit to adorn the robe
of love and righteousness.

At the end, my fellow Brethren,
he unveiled the truth
in wise sayings and parables.

Death quaked and was enraged
by itself and its Archons,
the dark powers, male and female gods,
archangels, and Earth's rulers.

Christ revealed the secret mysteries
but legalists soon dug his grave;
they condemned him as irreverent
unlawful and defiled.

On the third day he raised himself
from the dead, and as Saviour unveiled
the truth that gives Life to the All.

Those in heaven conferred with
those in the world and the underworld
about what would happen in his Name.

They would say he's unborn,
though he's born;
that he doesn't eat or drink,
though he does;
that he's uncircumcised,
though he is;

that he's bodiless, though he has form;
that he didn't suffer, though he did;
that he wasn't resurrected,
though he was!"

"All the tribes of the nations will
learn truth from you, Melchizedek,
Great High Priest, teacher of Abraham,
the Prophet, about his promise
for a perfect, fulfilled life."

"I am also the Gamaliel, sent to
visit the people of Seth's offspring,
who are above all Aeons and
their essence.

I acclaim Jesus Christ, Son of God,
who visited Abel Baruch
that you might hear this truth from me;
opposing forces are unaware of him
and their own death.

I am here to tell these secrets,
unveiled for the Brethren.
He shared the Living Truth with
your children; he offered them up
as a sacrifice to the All.

But it isn't oxen you should
offer for sins of infidelity,

nescience and evil deeds,
for they don't reach
the Father of the All,
but firm faith is certain
for those baptised in the
waters that lie above.

So welcome that baptism
which is approaching,
as they pray for the children
of the Archons, angels,
and my Father's seed.

From which were born
gods, angels, men, nature,
the heavens, the world, underworlds,
and the enigma of the feminine.

Yet what we're told isn't the real
meaning of Adam and Eve;
when they ate from the Tree
of Knowledge, they stamped hard
on the Cherubim and Seraphim,
Earth's lords and Archons,
their children, and the secret

male and female qualities
in all nature.

But they denounced the Archons
for they were fit to receive
the sacred immortal light!

But I'll keep silent,
for we are the Brethren
who descended from the seed
of Adam, Abel, Enoch, Noah
and myself, named Melchizedek.

These who are elected
will never be condemned,
whether they're born from enemies,
friends strangers, relations,
reverent or irreverent.

All opposing forces, seen or
unseen, in the world, underworld
or the heavens, will wage war.

I as Saviour will conquer,
and those chosen will surmount all;
not by words alone but through God's
grace will we end spiritual death.

I was ordered to unveil these secrets,
but don't tell anyone unless it's ordained
that you should do so."

Suddenly this High Priest
Melchizedek praised God,
saying, "We must be grateful
while He is living through us!

His grace is boundless.
He has great compassion,
sending his angel of light
from the Aeons,
to unveil the way to end
ignorance and to lead us from
death to Eternal Life.

I am Melchizedek, High Priest
of our God Supreme!

I know I am the similitude of
Lord Jesus Christ, the truest High Priest
of God, sent to this Earth.

It's not a trifling matter
that Almighty God is with us
and His angels that dwell in the world.

I speak of the Great Sacrifice
that deceived Spiritual Death!
When Christ the Saviour died,
he linked his own sacrifice
with the tendencies that are
leading the people away,
the devilish demons of desire.

I offer myself to you as a
child of this sacrifice, together
with all those who're mine.

To you, your own Self,
the Father of the All,
and those you cherish,
who've advanced through you
and are awakened and alive.

As decreed by the Flawless Law
I shall speak my Name,
as I receive everlasting baptism
from the living waters. Amen!

Sacred are you, Father of All, who
exists yet doesn't exist, eternally;
holy are you, Abel Baruch and
Barbelo, Mother of Aeons, and
Doxomedon, first born of the Aeons,
Harmozel, the first Aeon,
Oriael, Daviethel, Eleleth and
Mirochierothetou, Chieftains of
the Aeonic Light, and my Self
as Jesus Christ, eternal.

Blessed be my testimony;
I speak now to end fear
and all that's connected with it,
that sphere of darkness in which
bleak voices and pains manifest,
clothed with dread.

They spoke to me and said,
'Melchizedek, we've been led astray
from worship, faith and prayer.

We're of your primal stock,
yet didn't heed your priesthood,
having heard the wiles of Satan,
who exists in this Aeon and
seduces mankind.'

I, Melchizedek, answered,
'As your Saviour, I cast Satan
down so that you could all
be saved, yet you crucified me;
but as a corpse, from three
on sabbath eve 'til nine,
I rose from the dead.'

I was welcomed by my Father,
who said, 'Be brave Melchizedek,
once high priest of the Archons.

Your foes that declared war,
you're victorious over them!
You've vanquished them.

Don't reveal this to anyone
still identified physically
with their body, unless it is
commanded that you do so!'"

When the 'Brethren of the Rebirth
of Life' heard this great message
they were transported to realms
high above the heavens!

THE GOSPEL OF
PHILIP

An early Greek, Valentinian collection of Jesus's
sayings to his disciples. Many refer to the profound
sacramental mysteries of Baptism, Anointment, the
Eucharist and the Bridal Chamber.

A slave yearns to be free but he doesn't
hope to inherit his Master's house.
A boy isn't only a son, but in time
will lay claim to his father's estate.

Those who crave to be heirs of
the dead are already spiritually dead
and will inherit death.

Those who seek to be heirs of
the living are spiritually alive
and will inherit what is both
alive and dead.

The dead inherit nothing,
yet if they inherit what is living,
they'll gain Eternal Life.

A true Christian never dies
for he has not lived in vain,
to inherit spiritual death.

He who has great faith in Truth
has found the Real Life; this man
dares dying to his own Self,
to be truly alive.

Since Lord Jesus Christ came
the world has been recreated,
cities established, the dead buried.

When we were Jews we were fatherless
and had only an earthly mother.
Now, as Christians, we enjoy both
the heavenly Father and the divine Mother.

Those who sow in the hard winter
reap in glorious summer.
This world is a harsh winter;

summer is the eternal realm.
Let us sow now, in this wintry world,
so we may harvest in the splendid summer.

It is unworthy to pray
for boons in this winter.
Wait, for the summer
that will follow.

If a fool harvests in winter
he'll tear out the good he has
and be like a barren Sabbath;
Christ came to hold some in debt
and to release others from usury.

Those who were exiled,
he ransomed and made his own,
to set them apart; he pledged
them according to his Will.

When he came, he willingly
sacrificed his life, for it had
already been determined,
before this world was created.

He came first to redeem
it as it had been pledged.
It had fallen into the hands of
devilish demons and was imprisoned;
but he came to save both the
wicked and the good.

Light and darkness, life and death,
right and left, are inseparable twins.

For the good are not wholly good
nor the wicked wholly wicked,
nor is life merely life,
nor death merely death;
each will return to its primal source.

But those who transcend these
apparent opposites are eternal;
worldly names are full of deceit
and delude our minds.

They muddy the distinction
between right and wrong
with words like father, spirit, son,
life, light, resurrection and church.

In the eternal world there
are no such deceptions.

One Name is never uttered,
the Name the Father gave His Son.
For the Son couldn't have become
the Father unless he knew His Name.

Those who know this
Name never speak it.
Truth brought names into
being for our sake.

The dark powers wanted to
deceive man, to confuse his
relationship with the truly good.
They took good names and gave
them to the bad, so that with these
names they might bind them.

But through grace they remove them
from the bad and restore them to the good;
these dark forces wished to steal man's
freedom and enslave him.
These powers obstruct man's

salvation, for if man is saved,
animal sacrifice would end.

Before Christ there was no manna.
Just as Eden had many fields to feed
flocks but no wheat to feed Man.

Man used to munch like the beasts,
but Christ, the perfect Man,
brought manna from heaven so
Mankind could be fed by the spirit.

The dark powers imagine
it is by their own self will
that they do what they do;
yet the Holy Spirit secretly does
all through them, as it wills.

Truth which lives since the
beginning is sown everywhere;
many see the sowing,
few know the reaping.

Some claim that Mary's
conception was immaculate.

They're mistaken; women cannot
conceive from the Holy Spirit,
which is feminine.
It means that Mary wasn't
defiled by dark powers,
which defile themselves.

Jesus said to his disciples,
"Bring gifts to your Father's house;
don't steal from there."

Jesus is our Lord's secret name,
Christ is his revealed name.
In Syriac it is Messiah.
The Nazarene is he
who reveals the hidden.

Those who claim our Lord
first died then ascended, are wrong!
He ascended, then died.

No one hides a precious jewel
in a large container, but often
we have thrown many things into
a small worthless box.

The soul is precious, but not its flesh;
some fear they'll rise up naked
and wish to ascend fully robed,
but they don't see that those clothed
only by flesh are naked and ashamed.

In Corinthians it states:
 "Flesh and blood shall
not inherit the Kingdom."
What cannot inherit is the body alone;
what will inherit is that which belongs
to Jesus and his holy communion.

In John's Gospel, Jesus says,
"He who will not eat my flesh
and drink my blood has
no life in him."
His flesh is the Word,
his blood is the Holy Spirit.
He who receives these
has real food, drink and clothes.

It is necessary to ascend
through the Word of God,
for All is contained in that.

In this world those with clothes
are better than those in rags;
in the Kingdom of Heaven
God's robes are superior
to the souls that wear them.

It is through fire and water
that the world is purified:
the visible by the invisible,
the open by the hidden.

Much is hidden in the visible:
water in flowers, fire in
baptismal oil and balsam.

Jesus won them by cunning
for he did not appear as he really was,
but in a form that they could see.

To the great he seemed great,
to the little he was little,
to the angels he was an angel,
to men he was a man.
So his Word was hidden from all;

some indeed saw him and imagined
they were seeing themselves.

When he came to his disciples
in splendid glory on the Mount
of Olives he wasn't small;
he became great and made his
disciples great so they could
see him in his greatness.

On that day he said in gratitude,
"You who have united perfect light
with holy spirit, unite us with the
angels as well.

Don't scorn the Lamb; without him
it's impossible to know the King.
No one may visit the King without
robes of light.

The Heavenly Man has many
more sons than the earthly;
Adam's sons soon die,
but the sons of the Perfect Man
don't die, and are ever reborn.

The Father creates a son,
but the son hasn't the power
to create another.
He who has been reborn is
unable to bestow regeneration,
so the son wins brothers but not sons.

All men and women in this world
are born naturally, but those reborn
in God are nurtured by heaven.
It is by the divine kiss of grace
that the Perfect are reborn;
we also embrace each other to aid
conception by one another's grace."

Three walked with Christ:
Mary, his mother;
her sister, also Mary;
and Mary Magdalene.
All three were called Mary.

Father and son are single names,
omnipresent, above and below;
in the concealed and the revealed

the Holy Spirit is dual:
it is in the revealed below and
in the concealed above.

Some holy men are
served by sinister powers,
deceived by a spirit into the belief
that they're serving an ordinary man.

A disciple asked Jesus for something
from this world. He answered,
"Ask your mother. She'll bring you
things which belong to another."

The apostles said to the disciples,
"May our sacrifices contain salt!"

They called Sophia, the
Divine Wisdom, "salt".

Without "the savour of salt",
no sacrifice will be acceptable.
Sophia is childless, so she is
termed a "grain of salt".

Wherever they manifest in their
own path, the Holy Spirit and her
offspring will be fecund.

What the Father owns,
He gives to the son when
he arrives at manhood.

Those who've fallen away
yet are reborn by the spirit
may drift because of the spirit.
So by the same exhalation,
fire blazes and is extinguished.

Echamoth means wisdom of death;
one who knows death is termed
"the lesser wisdom".

There are tame beasts like cattle,
mules, dogs and sheep, but wild beasts
live mainly in the desert.

Man ploughs his field with
the aid of the ox, and from
tame beasts he's fed.

The Perfect Man ploughs
through his subdued powers,
preparing for all to come into Being.

Thus the world is established
through good and evil, right and left.

The Holy Spirit shepherds
us and rules all powers:
tame, wild and unique.
He hedges us in so we cannot stray.

Adam was created to be beautiful,
but Cain was not worthy.
Adultery followed murder;
he was the snake's child.

God is a Master Dyer,
His good and true dyes
dissolve with the robes they dye.

His dyes are immortal
by means of His colours;
first, He dips with water.

It's impossible to see what exists,
unless one becomes similar.

But the worldly man sees
the sun without being a sun;
the same with heaven and earth.

If you know the Spirit
you become the Spirit;
if you know Christ
you become Christ-like;
if you know the Father
you become as the Father.

The worldly see the All but
fail to know their own Self;
through Truth you learn
to know your Self;
what you know you become.

Faith accepts, love bestows.
None can receive without great faith.
No one can truly give without love;
he doesn't seek gain from what he gives.

He who has received something
other than our Lord remains a Jew.

The apostles prior to
ourselves had names for him.
Jesus was first the Nazarean,
then Christ, and then the Messiah.

Messiah means both Christ
and "the measured";
Jesus means "redemption",
Nazarene "the truthful".
Both the Nazarene and Jesus
have been justly measured.

If a pearl falls into mud
it becomes dirty and spoiled,
but if it is washed in balsam oil
it becomes precious;
yet it is always valued
in the sight of its owner.
The Sons of God,
wherever they may be,
are also valued by their Father.

If you say "I'm a Jew,"
no one's impressed;
if you say "I'm a Roman,"
no one's depressed.
If you say you're a Greek,
a barbarian, a slave or a freeman,
no one's worried.

But if you say "I'm a Christian,"
people will quake with fear.

Would I were like that person
whose name they cannot bear to hear.

God consumes man,
egos are sacrificed before Him;
animals were sacrificed
to those who weren't God.

Glass goblets and pottery jugs
are both formed by fire;
if glass breaks it can be re-moulded,
but clay vessels are shattered,
for they came into being without breath.

A mule that turned a mill stone
walked a hundred leagues,
but when released it was still
on the same spot!

There are folk who make
pilgrimages without progress.

When dusk falls they see
neither city nor town,
man-made monuments
nor sights of nature,
powers nor angels;
fools suffer in vanity.

Jesus is the Eucharist;
in Syriac he's called Pharisatha,
"the one who is stretched out";
Jesus came to nail this world
to the Cross!

Jesus entered Levi's dye works;
he took seventy-two dyes and
threw them in the vat.

The cloths all emerged pure white.
He said, "The Son of Man
comes as a dyer."

The childless Wisdom
is mother of angels.
Of all his disciples he loved
his companion, Mary Magdalene,
the most, and kissed her.

The disciples asked,
"Why do you love her most?"
He answered, "When a blind and
sighted man are both in darkness,
they are equal.

When light dawns, he who can
see will know the light;
he who is blind will stay in the dark."

Jesus said, "Blessed be he who IS,
before he came into being,
for he who IS has always been
and always shall be."

Man's mastery is invisible,
and lies in the concealed.

So he controls animals who
are stronger in terms of the visible;
thus they survive.

But when he leaves,
they quarrel and fight,
kill one another and
become cannibals.

Now they can all eat because a
superior man has tilled the ground.

If someone dives deep into
the well of living water and
surfaces empty handed, saying,
"I am a Christian,"
he has only borrowed the
name with interest.

If he receives the Holy Spirit,
His Name is the gift.

He who accepts this gift
doesn't have to give it back,
but from those who borrow at interest,
payment is demanded.

This is the way this
mystery is experienced.
Marriage is also a great mystery!
Without it our world couldn't continue;
contemplate this relationship.

Marriage in imagination
and fantasy is a defilement.
Forms of demonic spirits
are male and female;
males unite with souls that dwell
in the female form of those
who are disobedient.

None can escape them,
for they delay those who do not
receive the male and female powers
of bride and groom.
They are received from the
reflected light of the bridal chamber.

When a loose woman sees a lone
man, she leaps on him to defile him.
Similarly, lechers, when they see
a lone beauty, they seduce, to defile.
But if man and wife are seen together,
the female cannot seize the man
nor can the man enter the woman.

So if this symbol and an angel
are united, nothing harmful
can penetrate man or woman.

He who is no longer "of the world"
cannot be delayed on the grounds
that "he was once in the world".

He is obviously beyond
the plagues of lust and fear;
he masters the mind and senses
and is above jealousy.
If the enemy comes to attack,
he'll be defeated by a higher power.

There are some who claim
to be faithful, just to vanquish

impure thoughts and feelings.
But if they're firm in the Holy Spirit,
nothing unclean can ever touch them.

Don't be afraid of the body,
but don't adore it.
If you fear, it will gain mastery;
if you adore, it will render you helpless.

So the pilgrim lives in the world,
in regeneration, or in between.

God prevent me from falling
in between two places;
there is spiritual death.

In the world there's good and evil;
its goodness is not wholly good,
nor is its evil wholly evil.
But there's an evil that is diabolic,
this "in betweenness".

While in the world, it is worthy
to seek and find regeneration,

so that when we leave the body
we are at peace and not left hanging
in the middle.

Many stray from the straight path;
be wise and don't "be of this world"
before you sin.

There are some who are impotent
in their will to act and procrastinate;
they miss the mark.

An apostle, in a vision,
saw many folk trapped in a fire.
The voice of the Lord
offered to save them;
they disbelieved, hesitated,
and all perished in the flames.

It's from fire and water that
spirit and soul come into Being.
It is from these elements,
and light, that the groom of
the bridal chamber comes to be.

The fire is the baptismal
anointing oil.

The light's form is white,
bright and beautiful.

Truth does not come
into the world without robes;
it enters through words and pictures.

Truth cannot be received
by the world in any other way.

There is rebirth and
an image of rebirth.
We are born again through
the image of "Resurrection".

The bridal chamber is the
image of "Regeneration".

Those who speak the names
of the Father, the Son and the
Holy Spirit, do so for you.

If we do not know them in the heart,
the name "Christian" will be removed.

But we receive the boundless
grace of the power of his cross.
This power the apostles
called right and left;
it transforms men from
mere Christians into a Christ.

The Lord performed all his
acts in mystery: baptism,
communion, redemption,
and in the bridal chamber.
He said, "I came to make
the below as the above,
the outside as the inside,
and to unite them all through
the Word and the symbol."

Those who claim,
"There's the heavenly man,
and one above him" are wrong.
There are two heavenly men:
one revealed, who is below,

and one who owns the hidden,
who is above.

It is better to say "internal and external
and what's outside the external".
That is the reason our Lord called
destruction the "outer darkness".

He said, "Enter the chamber of
your heart, seal the door then pray
to your Father who is in secret."

The Father is the one within
them all and is the perfection.

There's nothing else
beyond "That I am".

Before Christ, some came from
where they couldn't enter;
if they did go in, they couldn't exit.

Those who entered, Christ released;
those who came out, he returned.

When Adam was still with Eve
there was no death;
after separation death appeared.

If a man or woman regains
his or her former Self,
there'll be an end to death.

"My God, my God. Oh Lord,
why have you forsaken me?"
Jesus pronounced these words
on the cross as a mystery,
quoting from King David's Psalms.

The bridal chamber is not fit
for beasts, slaves and loose women.
It is for free men and the virginal.

By the Holy Spirit and Christ,
we're born again, through both;
we're baptised by the Spirit and,
when reborn, made One.

You cannot see your reflection
in a glass or pool without light.

Nor can you see reflected light
without a mirror or water,
so it is right to baptise
in light and water.
The light is the oil.

In Jerusalem there were
three temples for the sacrifice.
The one facing west
was named "Holy",
the south-facing temple
was the "Holy of the Holy",
the east-facing one
the "Holy of Holies",
where only the High Priest
was allowed.

Baptism is the Holy,
Redemption is the
Holy of the Holy;
the Holy of the Holies
is the bridal chamber.

Baptism contains
redemption and resurrection;

redemption happens
in the bridal chamber.

The veil was lifted so some
below could rise above.
Dark powers cannot see
those robed in Perfect Light.
They cannot be impeded by them.
We are enrobed sacramently
in this light by atonement.

If the female did not divorce the male
she would not die with the male;
his exile is the advent of death.
Christ came to heal this alienation.

The bride is reunited with her
groom in the bridal chamber and
can never be divorced again.

Eve separated from Adam
because they were not united
in the bridal chamber at the heart's core.
Adam's soul came into Being
through the breath of the spirit.

The mother was given,
his soul was taken and the spirit granted;
linked to spirit he spoke words
beyond comprehension.

Dark powers were envious for they
had missed the chance to enter
the wedding chamber.

Jesus came to the River Jordan
in the perfection of the
Kingdom of Heaven,
conceived before the All
and reborn anew.

Anointed, he anointed afresh;
redeemed, he redeemed his flock.

I must speak about the great mystery;
The Father of All married a virgin,
who descended, and fire glowed
upon their wedding day.

His visible body, the whole universe,
came into Being on that day.

He left the bridal chamber
as one who came into being
from groom and bride.
So Jesus established all
through these miracles.

It is best for each disciple
to abide in his peace.
Adam came into being
from two virgins:
the Spirit and the Earth.

Christ's birth came to heal
the evil from the Fall.
Two trees grow in Eden:
one bears beasts, the other mankind.
Adam ate from the tree of beasts.

He became like an animal,
so his offspring worshiped them.
Men make gods
and praise their creation.
What a man achieves
depends on his talents,
and his children.

They commence in ease,
but man is made in the image of
strength yet has children with ease.

In this world slaves serve the free;
in heaven, the free will minister to slaves.

Children of the bridal
chamber minister to the
children of their marriage.
The name of these offspring is peace.

They don't need form
because they have meditation;
they are abundant in their Glory.

Those who enter living waters
will bless them in his Name.

Jesus said, "So we shall
fulfil all righteousness."

Those who say they'll die first
and then rise again are mistaken.

If they do not receive
resurrection while alive,
they'll receive nothing when they die.

I, Philip the Apostle, said,
"Joseph planted a forest
because he needed wood.

He made a cross from his trees;
his son was crucified on that cross.

But the Tree of Life is at
the heart of that forest.

We press baptismal oil
from the olive,
and resurrection follows.

The world is a corpse eater
consuming dead animals;
all who eat that meat also die.

Truth is a Life consumer;
no one who feeds upon it will die.
Jesus brought such food.

The Garden of Eden is the
place where angels say,
'Eat this and don't eat that,
as you so desire.'
Where I eat, all is from
the Tree of Knowledge.
It destroyed Adam but can
now bring men back from death.

The Tree is the Law.
It's empowered to give
knowledge of good and evil.
It neither removes evil
nor establishes good,
but kills those who choose
disobediently.

God said, 'Eat this,
don't eat that,'
and death was begun.
The chrism, the oil of holy unction,
is superior to the ceremony
of baptism itself.
The word Christian is derived
from chrism and the name Christ.

The Father anointed the Son;
the Son anointed the apostles,
who anointed us.
He who has been anointed
owns the resurrection,
the light, the cross
and the Holy Spirit.

The Father anointed the Son
in the bridal chamber
of the heart's core;
the Son surrendered his will.

The Father was in the Son
and the Son in the Father.
This is the Kingdom."

Jesus said, "Some have entered
baptism and the kingdom laughing,
as if it was of little worth,
so, out they come."

The world came through error,
for the Creator wished it to be
immutable and immortal.

It failed to reach His aim;
things cannot be immutable
but His Sons are; no one can become
immutable without first becoming
His Son. But he who is unable
to receive cannot give.

The grail contains water and wine,
consecrated as His blood,
for which we give thanks.
It is filled with Holy Spirit
and is from the perfect man;
when we drink we receive
His perfection.

The living water is His body.
We must don the living man;
before we bathe in the living waters
we must strip bare so we can
wear the perfect man.

Horses sire horses, men sire men,
God sires a god.
Compare that with groom and bride
who come from the chamber.

There's no real Jew, but from
Judaism came Christianity;
these are the Chosen, the sons of man,
known in the world as the children
of the bridal chamber so they may
endure for life everlasting!

In this life, marriage between
husband and wife shows strength
offset by physical frailty;
in the eternal sphere
the form is not the same.

They are not separate;
both come from the one
strong enough to rise above
the heart of flesh.

It is needed to own the All,
to know one's Self.
If one doesn't know one's Self
it's impossible to enjoy what's owned;
those who've come to know
themselves enjoy what they own.

The ignorant will be unable
to delay the perfect man or see him.
To attain the right to enter the Kingdom
one must be adorned with his Light.

The true priest is totally holy,
for he has consecrated the bread;
by enlivening the water of baptism
Jesus rid man of death.

If we descend to those living waters,
we do not descend to death;
then we will not be recycled
into the world's spirit.
When this spirit blows
it brings a harsh winter;
when the Holy Sprit breathes,
glorious summer blooms.

He who knows the Truth
is free from sin,
but he who sins is its slave.

Truth is the mother,
knowledge the father;

those whom the world believes
to be sinless are free.

Knowledge of Truth
can make people proud;
real freedom is being free
from arrogance.

Love builds, but he who
is free often becomes her servant,
through love, of slaves,
unable to reach Truth.

Love never controls;
it doesn't claim this is "yours"
and this is "mine" but says,
"All is yours!"

Spiritual love is wine and perfume;
if those anointed come with
bad smelling ointment,
then they should leave.

The good Samaritan gave
wine and oil to the weak man;

his ointment healed because
love cures a multitude of sins.

A mother's child looks like her husband,
if he truly loves her; if he or she cheats,
the child resembles one of their defilers.
If the wife sleeps with her husband
but thinks only of her lover,
the child will look like him.

You who dwell with God's Son,
don't adore the world but love the Lord
so your offspring will be like Him
and not the world.

Man enjoys sex with a woman,
the stallion with a mare,
the bull with a cow;
so spirit mingles with spirit,
reason weds reason, light shares light.

If you're born a man or a woman,
a human being will love you;
if you become truly spiritual,
the spirit will love you.

If you become one with
He who dwells above,
saints in heaven will
kneel down before you.

If you become a beast, outside
and below the spiritual realm,
neither human, spirit, reason
nor light will love you;
the Spirit within, and above,
won't dwell in you;
you'll lose your Friend.

He who subdues his personal
will shall become free.

He who becomes free
by grace of his master,
but then barters himself back
to hard slavery of his personal will,
won't ever be free again.

If you're a farmer you need
earth, rain, wind and sun;
God as your Farmer requires you

to cultivate faith, hope, love
and Self Knowledge.
Faith is our fertile ground;
hope, our gentle rain;
love, the soft breeze;
Self Knowledge, the sunshine!
Grace descends to earth from heaven.

Blessed is the one who saved souls;
that one is Christ.
He came to earth and unburdened all
who had faith in him, the perfect man.
The Word of God tells us the
Saviour is beyond description;
No one else can achieve
so much, or comfort so many.

He comforts all, never causing sorrow
to those who take refuge in Him alone;
wickedness and guile cause distress.
The perfect man brings peace and love,
yet some are stressed by that notion.

There was once a farmer who
owned sons, slaves, cattle, dogs,

swine, corn, barley, grass and nuts.
He was a caring man;
he gave bread to children,
corn meal to slaves,
bones to dogs, acorns to pigs.

So it is with God's disciples;
bodily appearances won't mislead them.
They'll scrutinise each other's spiritual
condition and advise appropriately.

There are animals in human form;
when He sees what they are
He feeds them the right diet.
To slaves He gives basic lessons,
to children, detailed guidance.

Our Lord is the Son of Man and
his son is he who creates through Him;
The Son of Man can also give birth;
to create a creature,
to give birth to offspring.
He who creates strives for all to see;
He who brings rebirth toils in private
and is concealed.

Only a man and wife can
tell when they enjoy sex.
Marriage is a mystery;
if there's mystery in the
wedlock of impurity,
how much more mystery is there
in the purity of the bridal chamber?

The sacred marriage is not carnal;
it is without desire and subject
to God's will, not from darkest night
but from brightest light.

When sex goes public, it's prostitution.
The bride can play the whore,
to be defiled by a lecher if she leaves
the bedroom and is seen.

Let the true wife confide only in
her parents, and friends and family
of the groom; they are permitted
to enter the bridal chamber.
The rest must pray only to hear
her voice and enjoy the perfume
of her ointment; let them feed from

table crumbs like puppies.
Brides and grooms belong
to the chamber;
no one should see them together
until they're like them.

Abraham was circumcised,
teaching that it is right to
admonish the flesh.

Providing man's inner parts are
protected, they'll labour and live;
once exposed, they'll stop!
If a man's intestines are opened up,
he'll die.

The same with a tree.
While the root is covered,
it will shoot and grow;
if it's exposed, the tree will wither.
It is so with all birth in this world.

If the root of wickedness
lies hidden in the dark
it waxes strongly;

when exposed to the light
of awareness it perishes.

That is why Matthew writes,
"Already the axe is laid
at the root of the trees";
it will not only cut the trunk
but also sever the root.
Jesus pulled up the root
of worldly sinfulness;
prophets partly did his work.

Each one of us must dig down deep
within ourselves and find the root
of this evil egotism in the heart,
so it will perish.
If we ignore this root,
more poisonous fruit
is produced in the heart;
it becomes our task master
and enslaves us, forcing us
to do what it desires.

It is powerful until seen and is active;
ignorance is the mother of all evil;

It will end in death!
For those who come from this,
iniquity will cease to exist.

When all the Truth is revealed
then man may be perfected.
Truth, unlike ignorance, while latent
is at rest, but when revealed
is stronger than the foe.
It brings freedom!
John wrote, "Truth
will set you free."
Ignorance is slavery,
Self knowledge is liberation.

If we know Truth,
its blossom will flower in
our hearts and bring salvation;
at the moment we're a mere
appearance in creation.

We say that the strong are held in
respect as great people and the
reviled are the weak, who are despised;
but the truth is different

and revealed in a symbol.
The bridal chamber is concealed;
it is the holy in the Holy.

The bridal veil hides how
God commands His work;
when unveiled, this house
will be destroyed.

The Godhead will retire,
not to the Holy of Holies
for it will not mingle
with the pure light
and flawless perfection.
It will rest beneath the
arms of the cross;
an ark will be their refuge
when the deluge descends.

The true priests may
enter within the veil
with the high priest;
the veil was not open only
at the top for then it would be
closed to those below.

It was not open only at
the bottom for then it would
be closed to those above.
It was open from top to bottom.
Those above revealed to
those below, so we could know
the mysteries of Truth.

Truth is what is held in great
respect and is really strong!
We enter bowed in weakness;
we are humble compared with
God's great power and glory.
His power and glory surpass
all power and glory.

Divine perfection is revealed
with the concealed secrets of Truth.
The Holy of Holies opens;
we are invited to the bridal chamber.

Hidden wickedness is now
less effective, but not cleansed
from the seed of the Spirit;
many may still be slaves of evil.

When revealed, the perfect light
will shine on all; all those within
its rays will be anointed and receive
baptism of the chrism.

The slaves shall be free
and the prisoners redeemed!

Matthew wrote, "Every plant
my Father in Heaven has not
planted shall be plucked."

The exiled will return to
unity and be fulfilled.

All who enter the bridal
chamber will light the light
as at night weddings.

But the mysteries of the
marriage are perfected by day,
not at night; an eternal day
that never sets.

All who become sons of the
bridal chamber will receive the light;
they'll be invisible and free
from torment, even in this world.

When he departs,
he'll have known Truth
through these symbols;
The world has become Eternal,
and is perfect for him.

This is how truth is given;
not hidden in darkest night
but revealed in brightest day
of holy light!

POIMANDRĒS

OR

THE POWER AND WISDOM OF GOD

A famed Gnostic work by the legendary Hermes
Trismegistus. After an Angelic Revelation, he
describes the mysteries of Creation, the Destiny of Man
and the Soul. The Tract concludes with an important
Gnostic Sermon and a devotional Prayer.

FROM *the Hermetica Tract I*

Once, while meditating
on "what is", my soul soared,
my senses stood firm, like those
of a man drunk with sleep,
from too much food and
physical exertion.

A huge Being of limitless
size appeared, called my name
and said, "What do you wish to

[124]

hear, see, learn and know from
your comprehension?"

I asked, "Who are you?"

"I am Poimandres,
Being of Kingship,
mind of Gnosis.
I know all your needs,
I'm with you everywhere."

I replied, "I want very much
to learn about life, its nature,
and to know God."

He answered, "Remember
all you care to know;
I shall teach you."

Suddenly he was transformed
into brightest light.

From this vision,
radiant, clear and joyful,
I felt wide open.

I enjoyed this state.

After a time darkness
descended, fearful and dense,
coiling serpent-like.

Then the darkness
seemed to liquefy vigorously,
emitting grey smoke.

It roared unspeakably.

Then a voice like the
crackle of fire spoke:

"Have you understood
the meaning of your vision?"

"No doubt I'll come to
know its meaning," I said.

"I am that Light, mind of
Gnosis, and God.

'That' which was, before
water issued from the night.

The illuminating Word
that comes from Gnosis
is the son of God."

"Proceed," I said.

"What you need to know,
is 'That' within you,
which sees and hears,
and comes from God's Word.

Your Self is the Father,
They're not separate,
their union is life."

I expressed my thanks
for this revelation.

He continued to speak,
"Understand and recognise
this Light behind and
within your mind."

He then gazed into my
eyes for some while.
I horripilated.

When he raised his head
I saw the Light of numerous
powers and an infinitely
radiant universe.

This fire, powerful yet
restrained, was held in place.

I was terrified, but he
addressed me once more.

"In your mind you've
witnessed archetypal form:
the primordial, pristine principle
that IS, before birth and death."

"What about the natural elements?"
I asked, "How have they arisen?"

"From God's wisdom,
which, absorbing the Word and

seeing the beauty of the potential,
actualised it, creating a universe
through its own elements
and myriad souls.

This 'nous' which is God is
androgyne, being both life and light.

By so uttering,
He gave birth to another mind,
a skilled craftsman,
Lord of fire and spirit.

He created seven Lords,
the planets who ruled
the sensual worlds.

Their government was called Destiny;
from the elements whose gravity
plunges downwards.

The Word soared
to create the skill of nature,
linking this craft with the craftsman.
This mind with the Word,

drew whirling circles,
turning from an endless beginning
to a beginningless end.

The circles created living
creatures, animals and beasts.

From the wind flew winged
birds of glorious plumage,
and insects with rainbow wings.

Water brought scaly fish
and monsters of the deep.

Gnosis, Father of All,
life and light, created Man,
whom he loved like his own son.
Man was fair, created
in the image of his God.

Enamoured by His own form,
God granted him all His craft skills.

So the Father allowed man
to exercise his power,

entering with permission
the craftsman's sphere.

He learned well and yearned
to break through the outer ring
of the spherical realms
and keep to the rule,
of one given power over fire.

Thus having authority over the
world of souls and dumb animals,
he pierced the vault and peered
through the cosmic framework,
revealing to lower nature
God's fair form.

Nature laughed with love
when she saw his beauty
and splendid energy.

In water she saw the
reflection of his noble shape
and its shadow on the Earth.

When Man saw his form
so mirrored, he fell into self love
and inhabited this imagination.

Nature then embraced
her newly Beloved
with welcoming arms.

Thus man is twofold:
mortal in body, immortal in
essence, subject to fate.

He's above the cosmic
framework, yet is its slave.
He's tireless because he
emanates from that One
who is indefatigable.

This is the mystery of
Gnosis, kept secret until now.

When nature consummated
her love with Man,
she bore seven babes,
androgyne and exalted,

like the seven planetary
Lords of the spheres."

Poimandrēs paused.
I interrupted and said,
"Pray please continue,
I long to learn more!"

He replied, "Be quiet,
I've yet to complete
my discourse.

I will tell you about her births.
Earth was feminine;
oceans and rain fertilised her.
Fire was the force of maturation.

Nature took spirit from ether
and bore more bodies
in man's form.

From Life and Light
came soul and mind.
All things in the sensual worlds
remained until the cycle ceased.

When the cycle ended,
the ties between all
were unfastened
by Divine Wisdom.

Living beings were split
into two halves, male and female.

But God ordered them to multiply
and to recognise their immortality.
And for many that desire is the
cause of their spiritual death.

Then providence ordained
sexual intercourse,
so all creatures multiplied.

The one who recognised
his true Self reached the
chosen Good.

But those still identified
with the body from desire
transmigrated to the darkness
of continuous rebirth."

I enquired what wrong
they had committed,
that they were deprived
of immortality.

He rebuked me, saying,
"You talk like a fool who doesn't
reflect on what he's heard.

Try and consider why they
deserve this form of living death."

I answered, "Because what
first appeared in each body was
dreaded darkness, born of the watery
nature from which death drinks."

"Yes, you've understood,
but why does this comprehension
lead a man towards God?"

I answered his question.
"Because the Father of All,
being Light and Life,
made man in his own image."

"You are correct!
Life and Light are God,
the Father from whom
Man emanates.
So contemplate this well
and you too shall
rise from the dead."

"However," I replied,
"God said the man who is mindful
should Self remember.
But surely all people have a mind?"

He rebuked me sharply.
"Hold your tongue.
Enough talk. Listen!
I my Self, I Am,
ever present to the blessed,
good, pure, aware,
compassionate, holy.

This Presence of the Self
becomes an aid.
They soon apperceive
this basic Recognition.

They worship their Father
with love and gratitude,
praising and chanting
hymns devotedly.

Before physical death
they learn detachment
from the dire effects
of lascivious lust.

I AM, as their Self,
will not permit these
defects to harm them.

As their friend and door keeper
I forbid entry to those with
shameful habits.
From these I keep due distance:
the evil, jealous, greedy,
violent, irreverent.

Those who yield to this lust,
a demon wounds with burning
coals and arms with pride so
greater vengeance may befall.

Such a victim never ceases
craving carnal concupiscence,
suffering in darkness so he's
tormented and the fire increases."

"You've taught me well.
Please tell me more about the
Ascent, and how it happens."

He graciously replied,
"In renouncing the gross
body, you hand yourself over
to transformation and the
old form goes.

The wicked demon
to whom you gave
your temperament
becomes powerless.

The body's senses rise up
and return to the Source,
separating and remingling
with His original energy.

The old feelings and cravings
return to irrational nature,
and the regenerated Man
is reborn through the spheres.

At the first, he renounces
getting and letting go;
at the second, evil inclination.

At the third,
illusion and delusion.

At the fourth, his usurping,
cardinal, egotistic arrogance.

At the fifth,
wilful presumption
and jeopardising bravado.

At the sixth,
greed, avarice, miserliness,
springing from passion for wealth
and perishable possessions.

At the seventh,
all deceit, betrayal, guile,
and calumny, lurking in ambush.

Then, stripped naked of the
old man, he enters the sphere
of Sophia, Divine Wisdom.

He has restored his own natural
power, and along with the Elect
worships his Father.

All those present rejoice
in His Presence.
And being His friend
he finds powers beyond
this sphere, and praises God
with a new song.

His hymn rises to his Father
and he surrenders himself
to God's almighty will
and enters into Him.
This is the ultimate Good
of Self Knowledge.

Why do you hesitate?
Hasten and become a guide
to the fit, so mankind
might share God's salvation."

As he was speaking
he renewed himself from
the Source and sent me forward,
empowered, and informed on
the universal nature and the
supreme vision; after I had given
thanks to my Father of the All.

I then proclaimed
to my fellow beings
the beauty of holiness
and Self Knowledge.

"Oh, poor, blind people,
who've seduced yourselves
by drunkenness, spiritual sloth
and ignorance of God.

Sober up! Put an end
to your evil malaise;

you're all hypnotised,
as if in a lunatic dream."

When the people heard
they gathered round,
and I repeated:
"Why have you committed
spiritual suicide when your
birthright is Eternal Life?

You who've flirted with crude
lies and partnered stupidity,
reflect, repent!

Abandon corruption
and degeneration.
Take your rightful place
in immortality!"
Some, in the grip of death,
moved on, mocking and scoffing.

But those who yearned
for enlightenment prostrated
themselves at my feet.

I then became their guide,
teaching salvation.
And I sowed the seeds
of higher wisdom, and
they drank from living waters.

When dusk fell I led them
in praise of our Almighty God,
and they retired.

Within myself I acknowledged
Poimandrēs' love, and I rejoiced.

My body's sleep became
my soul's temperance.
Closing my eyes
became real vision;
my silence was filled
with beatitude.
This happened because
I had listened attentively
to his Word of Kingship.

I had arrived, inspired by
the divine breath of Truth.

So I sing praises to the One God,
with all my heart, with all my soul
and with all my might!

"Holy is God, Father of the All.
Seated in your own power,
who yearns to be known
by his own children.

Who by your Word has created
all things precisely as they are.

The whole of nature
is your reflected image.

You're stronger than all forces,
superior to all excellencies.
The Supreme Perfection!

We can only meet
You in silence:
the unspeakable, unsayable,
inscrutable, unknowable.

Accept our sacrifice of
the hearts and souls that
cleave to You.

Grant my prayer, that I don't
fail in the Self Knowledge
that befits my True Nature.

Give me the strength and I
shall enlighten those trapped
in the snare of ignorance:
the brothers and sisters of my race,
Your sons and daughters!

This is my Faith.
I walk on victoriously
to Life and Light.

Blessed are You my Father.
I am Your slave and wish to
aid Your work of holiness,
since You've blessed me
with great wisdom!"

THE APOCALYPSE OF THE GREAT POWER

An early Coptic Gnostic Narrative telling of Creation,
Divine Justice, Mercy and the conflict between
Good and Evil. It concludes with a dramatic apocalyptic
vision of the world's end and the salvation of Souls.

He who'll know
our One Great Power
will not be seen.
Its fire won't kill him,
but will purify and burn up
all his worldly goods.

All who see my shape
shall be saved,
those from seven days
to one hundred and
twenty years old.

I instructed some to collect
all that's been revealed as

the book of our Great Power.
So that power may inscribe
their name in its radiance
and their labour end.

That they may be purified,
dispersed and self-abnegated,
so they may meet in that sphere
where no one else can see.

But you can see me and make
your home in our Great Power.
Comprehend what's happened to Be,
so you can understand what endures
and what form the Aeon takes.

Why not enquire
diligently into that?

Think how vast is the ocean,
beyond measure and comprehension,
in beginning and end.
It maintains the world,
and wafts the winds
where gods and angels dwell.

But for he who is above all this
there's awe and light,
and to him my book is unveiled.

I have written it as a service
for created human beings,
for it is impossible for any man
to be firm without knowing The One.

Nor can an Aeon endure without Him.
Only he who knows his own Self
can contemplate "That" in purity.

Know "That Spirit" and his heart.
He sacrificed himself for mankind
so they may receive perennial life;
since He possesses Life within
Himself, He's able to give it to all.

Then night and hell together
conspired to steal my fire,
and this darkness will not return
to those who are truly mine.

Its eyes cannot stand my Light;
after spirits and waters moved,
what was left came into being,
the entire Aeon of Creation
and its forces.

Fire issued from them and
the Power descended in the
middle of their energies and
wished to see my similitude,
so the Soul became its duplicate.

This is the creation that
came into existence;
before emerging, it was blind,
for the fleshly Aeon entered
gross bodies and they were
granted length of days.

For when they self-corrupted
and penetrated the flesh,
the fleshly father, water,
revenged himself when he learnt

that Noah was saintly and fit,
and that the fleshly father keeps
even the angels in servitude.

And Noah taught righteousness
for one hundred and twenty years,
and no one paid due attention
until he built an ark of teak
and his chosen flock took refuge.

When the flood descended,
Noah and his sons were saved.
For if their ark hadn't been
meant for man and his animals,
the deluge wouldn't have happened.

In this way Noah decided to rescue
the gods, angels and spiritual
powers, their magnitude, their
manna and manner of living.
He moved from that Aeon
and fed them in eternal realms.

The fleshly judgement
was pronounced;

only the Creation of
the Power remained.

The next Aeon was the small,
psychic one, which when mingled
with the physical gave birth in souls
and polluted them.

Its offspring were rafts of wrath,
jealousy, ill will, guile, disdain,
strife, mendacity, wicked advice,
depression, hedonism, lowliness,
corruption, falsity, sickness,
bad judgement and depravity,
all of which were craved according
to their particular pernicious lusts.

You who are fast asleep,
dreaming the dream of life,
stir yourself, awaken
and attentively search within!

Savour and enjoy true
nourishment, teach the Word
of God from the fountain of life.

Put an end to wicked appetites,
yearning for Anomoean doctrine
and wicked falsity that lacks
a firm foundation.

The Fire Mother was powerless;
she set light to the soul and the world,
scorching all its constructions.
Even its Arch-Mentor died.

And if there was nothing
left to ignite, she'd set light
to herself and be bodiless,
incinerating gross matter
until she removed all evil;
this is the psychic Aeon.

A man will appear who
knows the Great Power;
he'll accept and understand me;
he'll drink his Mother's milk,
preach in parables and pronounce
the next Aeon as he announced
the fleshly Aeon as Noah.

Regarding his words,
he spoke in seventy-two tongues;
he opened heaven's doors
and shamed Hell's tyrant!
He awakened the dead
and destroyed Satan's power!

Then turmoil broke loose.
The Archons were enraged
and wished to capture him and
hand him over as a prisoner
to the tyrant of Hell.

They tempted one of his
disciples and set fire to the
soul of one named Judas, who
delivered him to the temporal power.

They seized and tried him,
bringing down Justice upon
themselves, delivering him
to Sasabeck, Governor of Hell,
for nine brazen shekels.

This Saviour prepared himself
to descend and shame them,
but Sasabeck captured him.

But he discovered that this
Saviour's true nature
couldn't be seized to hand
over to the Archons.

"Who is this, what is this?"
he enquired. "He's destroyed
the Aeonic law; he's from the
Logos of Life's Great Power.
He's triumphed over the Archonic
rule and they are powerless."

The Archons tried to find
out what had happened.
They failed to see this was
the beginning of their end
and the ancient Aeon would change.

The Sun eclipsed, all was darkness,
wicked spirits became fearful.
They saw he'd soon rise up and

the signification of the new Aeon
would be proclaimed
and old Aeons would vanish.

Those who know these events
will be blessed and will unveil them,
for they've known truth
and found heavenly peace.

Many will follow him
and toil in their own lands;
they'll travel and become scribes,
writing down his teachings.

These Aeons have now vanished;
So, how vast was the Aeonic
ocean that has gone?
What size are these Aeons?
How should mankind make
ready for the new Aeon?
How will they become steady,
deathless Aeons?

After teaching, the Saviour
announced the second Aeon;

the first disappeared
after he had preached for
one hundred and twenty years.

This is the ideal number
that is highly revered;
he made the western fringe
a wasteland and destroyed
the eastern edge.

This is written to inform
your offspring and all who
wish to follow our Great Logos
and his declaration.

Then the Archons raged,
as they burned,
shamed by their destruction.
They smouldered, waxing
wrathfully at this life.

Their towns were shattered,
their mountains quaked;
the vultures came
and dined on their dead.

The earth lamented
in grief with the people
and they despaired.

When these days were
over, evil arose again
until the end of the Logos.

The Archons of west and east
vowed to perform the task
of tempting men into sin.

They desired to annihilate true
teaching and words of wisdom
while encouraging falsehood.

The Archons assailed
the venerable teachings,
wishing to spread iniquity,
so they pretended to be worthy.

But they were impotent
because the corruption
within them was too great.

Then the Great Logos
became enraged and
wished to visit their land.

The time arrived, when he'd
grown from a babe to manhood,
and the Archons sent a deceitful
impersonator to steal his
knowledge of his Great Power.

They hoped to tempt him
to perform miracles,
to reign over the world
and lead mankind astray.

Then the impersonator would
teach circumcision and condemn
the uncircumcised Gentiles,
who are a true people.

He sent many false teachers
in advance of the time to come,
when he'll scour souls of purity
and make evil more effective.

The oceans will dry up,
the heavens will cease
sending morning dew,
the river springs will silt up,
the deep will be laid bare and wasted,
the stars made to wax large
and the sun extinguished!

Then the Great Logos, the Christ,
will retreat with all who know him
and enter the infinite light,
where there's no one of lustful
flesh to take them prisoner.

They will be free and holy;
nothing will assail them.
He shall guard them
as they wear sacred robes
which fire cannot burn,
nor black night or fierce storm
cause their true vision to cease.

Then he'll vanquish the wicked;
they'll be punished and cleansed.

Their time of power will be confined
to fourteen hundred and sixty years.

When fire has destroyed all,
it will consume itself.
The work will be fulfilled;
compassion and knowledge will thrive!

The heavens will fall
into the deep, the sons
of materialism will die.
Souls will appear who have
been made holy through the
light of the Great Power which
is above all powers, infinite,
universal, "I AM," and
those who know me.

They'll dwell in the Aeon of
Justice and Beauty for they
are prepared in truth, having
worshipped inscrutable unicity
and known Him through His will,
which is in them as their own.

And all will be as mirrors
of His great light, shining and
finding rest in His peace.

He'll free the souls being punished
and they shall be purified.
All shall be purified.
They'll know the saints and pray
"Have compassion on us,
Great Power, who is superior
to all other powers."

For in the tree of life, those that
see evil will be made blind;
we'll not search for them
for they do not search for us
or have faith in us.
But they acted because
of the Archons and their Lords.

We have acted according to our birth
in the creation of the Archon of
Great Power which brings Law,
and we're the immutable Aeon!

THE SOPHIA OF
JESUS CHRIST

This complex revelational discourse given by the
Resurrected Christ describes invisible celestial regions.
Christ is the Incarnation of the Gnostic Saviour and
Sophia the female personification of Divine Wisdom,
an archetype of the Great Mother.

After his resurrection from the dead,
Christ's twelve disciples, with the
seven women, went to the Mountain
of Divination and Joy at Galilee.

They were concerned about the
substratum of the universe,
its plan, the power of the State,
Divine providence, and the Saviour's
hidden way towards them.

When suddenly he appeared,
not in his familiar form but as an
invisible, almost palpable, spirit.

His similitude resembled
a vast angel of pure light.

I must not describe his plenitude;
no human mind could bear it,
only pure souls.
It was that on which he'd
preached, at the Mount of Olives.

He said, "My peace be with you,
I hand it to you all."
They were amazed and quaked.

Jesus laughed and said,
"Why are you so concerned.
What are you seeking?"

Philip answered,
"We are questing for the
knowledge underlying substance
and the Divine plan."

Jesus replied, "I wish you
to understand that all born into
this world from its beginning until now,

being earth bound, although enquiring
about God, haven't yet found Him.

The wisest have pondered on the
ordainment of the world and its motion,
but they haven't found the Truth.

Ordainment is controlled threefold,
claim philosophers, who can't agree.

Some think it's self-motivated,
that it's Divine providence or fate.

It's none of these!
None are near the Truth
for they reason with
man's limited mind.

But I my Self, who emanates
from pure boundless Light.
I AM here, I know God.

I can tell you about the
precise nature of Truth.

What emerges from itself
is impure and self-generated;
providence lacks Wisdom
and fate lacks discrimination.

It's given to you to understand,
and whoever's fit will understand!
Not those conceived
through impure intercourse,
but He who's conceived
by the Primal energy is eternal
in the midst of mankind."

Matthew said, "Master,
nobody can find Truth except
through you, so pray tell us!"

Jesus answered, "He who is
beyond words is inscrutable,
not subject to mastery, from the
world's beginning until now.

Except for Himself alone and
anyone else He wishes to inform.

He who IS comes
from primordial Light;
I am that unborn,
deathless Saviour.

Since He isn't subject to
any object, He is nameless;
He that is named is the
notion of another.

He is formless but has a strange
representation, like no one else,
superior even to the universal.

He sees all sides and knows
His own Self, from and by Himself,
boundless, unknowable,
deathless, beyond comparison.
He is immutable goodness,
perfect, without flaw, immortal.

He knows His own Self
beyond measure, leaving no mark,
pristine without blemish,
ever blessed, The Father of All".

Philip asked, "Master,
how did He come to the Elect?"

Jesus replied, "Before anything
can be seen from what is visible,
it must be known that the sovereignty
and glory are with Him.

He contains All,
while nothing contains Him.
He is all Wisdom, reason,
reflection and power.

All these forces are equal and
form the source of All.

The whole of mankind
from beginning to end
was known in his foresight,
for He is the boundless
unborn Father of All."

Thomas asked, "Lord,
how did these powers come to be
and why were they created?"

Jesus answered, "I come
from the limitless that I might
inform you about the All.

The Spirit who had this power
gave birth and created nature's forms,
so the great prodigality concealed
in him might be revealed.

Because of his compassion
and unconditional love,
he wished to bear such fruit
so he need not enjoy
his abundant perfection alone.

Reason reveals how faith
in unseen powers was found
in the seen and is owned by
the Unborn Father.
Whoever has ears to hear,
let him hear!

The Almighty King of the
Universe is called not just Father,

but also our Grand Father,
for He was the source
of all that was to come.

Seeing His own Self as
if reflected in a mirror,
He manifested,
representing Himself.

His similitude was the
Divine Self, and Father;
the opponent of all
that opposes.

Primordial, Unborn,
Self-existent, equal in eternity
with His own Light,
but greater in power.

Then there appeared myriad
self-generated souls,
equal in eternity and force,
whose kind is named the
'Generation Without A Kingdom'.

These are they from whom
you've come, named mankind.
Sons of the unborn Father
whose similitude is within you.
Full of everlasting glory,
unspeakable joy and
infinite celebration!
This wasn't realised before
among all Aeons and their worlds."

Matthew asked, "How was
man brought into Being?"

The Perfect One replied,
"He who always existed,
before the Universe was created
entered into eternity,
as the Self Originated Father,
full of effulgent light.

Then He willed His similitude
to become an almighty power.
Instantly the essence of that
pure light became immortal,
Androgyne Man.

So that through this immortality
man might attain Self Knowledge
and awaken from his deep sleep
of forgetfulness.

Through the grace of the divine
messenger, who'll be with you
'til the end, even midst this
spiritual poverty of thieves.

His bride is the Magnificent Sophia,
who first, through immortal man,
appeared as Divinity, the Kingdom
and the Father, the Self-originated,
who revealed all.

He formed a great Aeon
for his Sovereignty,
and as King reigned over the
universe of spiritual poverty.

He created gods, archangels
and innumerable angels
for his Kingdom of Light.

And the male triumvirate
that was in Sophia
brought forth God,
Divinity and the Kingdom.
He was Named God of Gods
and King of Kings.

Archetypal man has a
unique intellect, powers of
self-reflection, and reason.

His qualities are perfect and
eternal but his powers are unequal,
like a son to his Father.

The monad, the simple unity,
was primal in creation.
All that manifested was formed
and named by His Great Power.

The distinction between the born
and the unborn was made.
Now Eternal Man is full of
undying glory and holy joy;
his whole kingdom rejoices for ever."

Bartholomew asked,
"Why was he called Son of Man.
Who is Father to this Son?"

The Saviour answered,
"Primordial Archetypal Man
is creative, Self-perfected wisdom.

He meditated with his bride Sophia
and his first offspring was born,
an androgyne.

His male part is named
the Son of God.

His female part,
the Sophia,
Mother of the Universe.

Her name is Love;
the son is Christ
since he derived power
from his Father,
who created angels
from spirit and light."

His disciples said,
"Lord, tell us about Man
so we may know his glory."

Jesus replied,
"Whoever has ears to hear,
let him hear!

The first Procreator
or father is Adam,
eye of light, for he came
from radiant light
with His holy angels,
beyond speech
and without shadow.
Praising with great joy
their powers of reflection,
inherited from their Father.

The whole Kingdom of the
Son of Man, the Son of God,
is full of indescribable,
shadowless joy, constant
celebration and rejoicing
at his undying glory,

never known before
nor revealed in previous Aeons.

I came from that Primordial,
Self-originated, primal,
boundless light,
that I may tell you all."

His disciples asked once more,
"Tell us simply how they descended
from the invisible, the undying realms,
to the world that dies."

The perfect saviour said,
"The Son of man agreed with
Sophia, his consort.
He displayed a vast
androgyne light;
his male name is
Saviour of All.

His female name
is All Procreator,
Sophia Pistis.

All born into this world,
descending like a ray
from His radiant light,
are sent by the Almighty
to return eventually to Him,
and be ever protected.

The bondage of man's ignorance
tied him to Sophia's will so that
the whole world, in spiritual poverty,
could see its arrogance and blindness.

But I come from a realm above,
sent by the will of the Great Light
that escaped from this bondage.

I have stopped the pillage of thieves,
I have awakened that ray sent by Sophia
that my work might bear good fruit.

And through me men might be
perfected and not be defective,
unified through me, the Great Saviour,
so God's glory might be revealed.

Sophia felt justified, and her sons
determined to achieve honour and
glory and return to their Father and
understand the Word of masculine light.

You, my disciples, were called
by me that you might receive that
Light and free yourselves from
the power of dark forces.

Then the world will no more manifest
before you because of unclean
carnal intercourse and the fearsome
power that comes from lust.
You'll stamp upon all evil intent!"

Then Thomas asked,
"Lord, how many Aeons
are there that rise above
even the heavens?"

Jesus answered, "I praise you
since you enquire about the Aeons,
for your own source is in the limitless.

When what I've stated was revealed,
The Self Originator, the Father,
created twelve Aeons as spheres
for His twelve angels.

All these were perfect
and filled with goodness,
but a flaw in the female
portion appeared.

The first Aeon is the Son of Man,
the Primal Procreator,
the Saviour who is now come.
The second is Archetypal Man,
Adam, eye of light.

That which contains these is
that Aeon, subject to no other kingdom,
the everlasting boundless
Self-Originated Aeon of all Aeons.
The Aeon above the seventh
came from Sophia, the first Aeon.

Immortal man displayed his
Aeons, powers and kingdoms,

granting rule to all who manifest in him.
So they might fulfil their will
until the ending of the last matter
that hangs above chaos.

The Aeons agreed with one another
and displayed their greatness from
spirit with myriad brilliant lights.

In the genesis they were given names:
the first Aeon, the beginning;
the second, the intermediate,
and the third, the perfect.

The first was termed
Unification and Peace.
The third was called 'Congregation',
from the vast multitude that appeared
in the multitudinous.

So when the multitude congregates,
they come to the unification
termed Congregation,
from that same name,
which exceeds heaven.

The Congregation of the
eighth Aeon was androgyne,
part male, part female.

The male was termed
Congregation; the female, Life,
so it might be shown that from
the female issued Life, in all Aeons.
Each name was accepted
from the beginning!

Gods created from their
contemplation, lords,
archangels and angels.
Similitudes emerged with
substance, shape and name,
for all Aeons and worlds.

The immortals derive their
power from Immortal Man,
who is named Silence.

He, by ruminating without
words, established his
own sovereignty.

The Deathless Ones
created a great kingdom
in the eighth sphere.

With temples, thrones and
heavens for their own Kings.

All this happened by
the will of the Divine
Universal Mother."

Then the Apostles said,
"Lord, pray tell us about
those who live in the Aeons."

The Saviour replied,
"Hosts of angels, virgin spirits
and radiant lights were created
for their might and splendour.

They are free from
illness and frailty.
So all Aeons and heavens,
in the splendour of Immortal Man
and Sophia, were created.

All subsequent creation
followed this archetypal image,
in the heavens of chaos
and their dependent worlds.

All natures emerging from
primordial chaos are in
shadowless light, unspeakable joy
and unutterable celebration.

They are glorified in absolute peace
among all Aeons and powers.

All that I've said is to
aid you shine in light
even more than these!"

Mary asked, "Lord, from
where did your disciples come?
Where are they going?
What should they do?"

Jesus answered,
"Sophia the Mother,
and her husband,

wished to create all
without male intervention.

But by the will of
the Father of All,
that His infinite Love
might be made known,
He wove a veil between
the Immortals and all
that followed.

Each Aeon and chaos risks
that female imperfection
might occur and errors
may oppose her will.

These became the veil
of spirit from Aeons
above the Light.

A ray descended to God's
nether regions in chaos,
so their shapes might
come from that beam;
it's a judgement on the

Arch-Procreator,
called Yaldabaoth.

That ray revealed
their sculpted shapes
through His breath,
as living souls.

This spirit fell fast asleep
in the soul's ignorance.

Then it was warmed from the
breath of the male light and
attained the power of Reason.

Names were given to all in chaos;
this happened by the will of Sophia,
that Immortal Man might weave
special ropes, as justice for thieves.

He welcomed the breath
but, as a soul, he wasn't fit
to seize that power until
chaos was completed,
as ordained by the Archangel.

I've taught you all
about Immortal Man and
released the ropes of thieves
from his power.

I've shattered the doors
of the merciless ones
and subdued their evil intent
until they're ashamed
and struggle upwards
from dark ignorance.

That's why I've come!
So spirit and breath
might be united
and two become one.

From the first, ripe fruit
grows and rises up to Him
who is from the genesis,
in unspeakable joy and splendour.

All shall honour our
Father's Grace;
whoever knows about

the Supreme God who reigns
above the whole universe
shall stamp on their own death,
frustrate their evil inclination,
cut the knot of their ignorance,
awaken my grace and aid,
and trample over dark powers!"

These are the words spoken
by the Perfect Saviour,
Lord Jesus Christ.

He left his disciples everlastingly
in their spirit's holy joy,
and they went to teach
his living Gospel of God,
the everlasting unborn spirit.

Amen

HUMAN SUFFERING

A fragment by the famed Gnostic,
Basilides of Alexandria (second century AD), who
believed that the Will of God is Omnipotent and Good,
and that Suffering is a form of Divine Justice and
has a reformative value. He wrote many important
Gnostic commentaries on the Gospels.

Basilides said, "I have
faith that all who suffer have
missed the mark more than
they know, in this or another
life, and now shall come to
a beneficial end."

Paul told the Romans,
"Once, I lived separated
from the law."

He meant that before this
life he lived in a body not
subjected to God's law.

By the Divine grace
which directs them,
they may be reviled for irrelevant
crimes and not be compelled
to suffer as convicted criminals,
adulterers or murderers.

But instead they endure trials
because they are Christians,
which ameliorates their pain.

But even if an egotism
suffers without sin,
which is most unusual,
the torment isn't forced by
the conspiracy of some authority.

It's more like the wails
of a new-born babe,
who seems to be innocent.

THE GOSPEL OF
TRUTH

This powerful early Greek Gnostic Treatise
covers topics such as "The Quest for the Father",
the "Hope of Salvation" and the "Need for a Saviour".
All will help to redeem the Soul from its ignorance.

The Gospel of Truth is sheer
perfection and holy joy!

For all those who've received
their Father's grace by knowing
who He really IS.

Through the force of His Word,
which issued from the fullness
of the Godhead.

That is Christ,
who is in the heart of his Father,
with the sacred task he's been set,
to save and enlighten those in ignorance.

This gospel gives hope of certainty
for all who diligently enquire.

When the Whole went
seeking for the One
from whom All come,
the All was found to
be the Divine Self,
Almighty God, inscrutable,
indescribable, supreme.

Nescience had caused
anxiety and fear,
a smutty fog that made
people feel blind.

Error became potent
and, through folly, began
creating with force and beauty
a falsity of truth.

This wasn't an embarrassment
for the inscrutable, indescribable
Supreme; it was as nothing,
this angst, forgetfulness and guile,

for Real Truth is unchanging perfection.

From this fact, learn to hate error,
which lacked knowledge of the
source and dropped into dense mist,
regarding the Father,
forming illusion to frighten and
seize those beings existing in
the intermediate realm.

The Father didn't cause this error,
although all emanates from Him.

Knowledge came from Him,
that forgetfulness which causes error
might be destroyed.

The Gospel of Christ, when sought,
reveals the secret mysteries to those
purified through His grace,
enlightening all encased in darkness
through forgetfulness.

He pointed out the Way of Truth,
which he preached.

Error became enraged,
persecuted and attacked him,
but was nullified by his sacrifice.

Crucified, he became
a source of Knowledge
concerning his Father.

It didn't lead to annihilation
because his Way was practised.
Those who practised rejoiced,
discovering Him in themselves.

As for the inscrutable, unknowable
One, the Father, the Flawless One,
who created the All and contains the
All and whom the All always needs,
He held flawlessness within himself,
which He didn't pass on to the All;
He wasn't envious;
what envy could there possibly be
between Himself and the All?

For if the Age had received
His flawlessness, the All

wouldn't have returned
to the Father.

He holds their flawlessness,
granting it as a boon to those
who return to Him with perfect
knowledge of the Unity.

It is He who created the All;
in Him dwells the All;
All have great need of Him.

Our Father wills that the nescient
will eventually know and love Him.

Christ was teacher of All,
peaceful and at ease.
In houses of devotion he came
and spoke His Word.

Philosophers, wise in their
own opinion, tried to refute Him.
He defeated them for they
were ignorant, and in their folly
they came to hate him.

Children came, those to
whom knowledge of their Father
hadn't been forgotten,
and he strengthened them.

They learned about, they knew,
they worshiped the Father.

The living gospel of the Father was
inscribed on their hearts' splendour!

That which pre-existed in the
Father's will before His creation,
within His inscrutability.

That secret tome which
nobody could steal, for anyone
who stole it would perish.

Nobody among the faithful
would have been saved unless
this tome had been revealed.

The all-loving Christ was
long-suffering in bearing

the suffering of others,
until he received that tome,
since he knew his own death
would bring new life for the multitude.

When a rich householder dies
there's often a secret clause
in his will revealing his fortune.

So it was with the All
which dwelled secretly,
while our Father of the All,
from whom all space emanated,
remained unseen.

When Christ came,
he became the Gnosis
of that secret tome
and was crucified.

He revealed the tome of his
Father by his death on the cross.
Such a magnificent teaching!

He attracts his own death,
although Life Everlasting
is his robe of glory.

Having thrown off transient tatters,
he donned the cloak of durability,
which nobody could steal.
Having come to the vale of fear,
he walked through it.

Those who were naked and
unclothed through forgetfulness
gained understanding and flawlessness.
Then they taught the
truth from their hearts,
to those open to receive.

Those who were willing to learn
his doctrine are alive and are
inscribed in the book of life.

It is about their own Real Self
that they hear teaching,
receiving it from their Father
and turning inwards towards Him.

It is necessary that the All
shall aspire towards Him,
for the flawlessness
of the All is in Him.

If the aspirant has understanding,
the Father takes him back to Himself.

For he who is trapped in necsience
lacks, and what he lacks is crucial.

He needs that Self Knowledge
which will make him flawless.

For the flawlessness of the
All dwells in the Father;
they must turn inwards towards Him.

He chose them beforehand and
matured those who came from Him.

Those whose names He knew in
advance were summoned for the end.
Thus the names the Father
has uttered have understanding;

the names of the uncalled
remain nescient.

Those who stay in nescience
until the end are people of
forgetfulness and will vanish.
Why are these wretched ones
nameless and not summoned?

Only he who has the understanding
that descends through grace is called.
He listens, responds, turns within
and cleaves towards Him.

He acknowledges His call and
yearns to perform his Father's will;
he wishes to please Him and
is rewarded with peace.

Each name comes before Him,
knowing from where he came
and where he is going.

The Chosen knows, like a drunkard
who has returned to sobriety.

Christ has rescued
many from falsehood;
he has visited their hearts,
from which they had strayed.

Because of an abyss
they fell into falsehood,
the void which encloses a space
in which nothing is enclosed.

It was a miracle:
they were within the Father
while not recognising Him,
and they were able to walk on,
for they failed to understand or to
know the One in whom they dwelled.

If His will hadn't issued from Him
as revelation, the knowledge of
how His various rays harmonise
would have stayed in nescience.

This is the Knowledge of
the Book of Life He gave to
twenty-three Aeons at the end.

He showed how His sacred
letters are neither vowels
nor consonants, so that one
could read them and think
they were unwise.

Yet they are letters of Truth
to those who know how to read.

Each letter is a total conception,
like a whole volume, for they are
letters inscribed by the One!

Our Father composed them for
all Aeons so they would know Him.

His wisdom meditates
on His Word, His doctrine
unveils His knowledge.

Patience is its crown;
joy is in perfect concord.
His splendour uplifts that
which His will has unveiled.

His peace has taken it into itself,
His love has enrobed it,
His faithfulness has taken it to heart.

In this way the Word of
Almighty God the Father
advances into the All,
as the fruit of His heart's core
and the seal of His will.

It maintains the All, elects
them and absorbs its effect.
It purifies, leading them back to
Him and into the Divine Mother,
also to the Christ of infinite sublimity.

The Father unveils His heart,
the Holy Spirit.
He reveals what is secret,
His son, so through His grace
the aeons may know Him
and cease toiling in seeking Him,
but abide in Him,
knowing that is true peace.

Having remedied the lack
He destroyed the form,
the sphere in which He worked.

For where there's jealousy
and conflict, it's lacking;
but where there's Oneness,
there lies flawlessness.

The lack manifests because
our Father was unknown;
when He's known,
that will vanish.

It's like a man in nescience;
when knowledge comes,
nescience is dissolved.

Night disappears when dawn breaks;
lack dissolves in the flawlessness.

From that time on, form is
invisible and disappears in
mingling with the One.

Now its works lie
fragmented in time;
Oneness will become
flawless and in time make
all space the same.

He creates whomever and whatever;
He wills by bestowing name and form
and causes those that are born
to be unaware of their Creator.

Those yet to be born are as nothing,
but are in Him and wish to be born
when He wills; like in the time to come.

Before all manifests, He knows
what He'll create and destroy.

But His unborn fruit are ignorant
and can do nothing without His grace.

All space in our Father is
from the One, who created it
from nonexistence.

He who has no root has no shoot,
and although he imagines he has come
into existence, he will cease.

For he who doesn't truly exist
can never come into fullness
of flawless Being.

How then did he regard himself?
As one who comes into existence
like night-time shadows and ghosts.

But when the Light shines on his
fright he sees that he is as nothing.

So they were in ignorance
of their Father,
He being invisible to them.
Since through fear, turmoil,
imbalance, doubt and strife,
there were myriad delusions.

Imaginary souls lost in heavy torpor,
full of agonising dreams.

Either they're trying to escape
without help or they come
hunting after others.

Striking blows or receiving them,
falling from heights or flying in air.
Being slain without a slayer or
slaying their friends, covered in blood.

When those that suffer
these nightmares wake up,
they see them as nothing
for they themselves are nothing.

Such is the path of those who've
shed their nescience, like a dream
without substance.

The knowledge of their Father
comes as something of great worth,
like a glorious sunrise.

Each one lived as if in a deep
sleep when ignorant, and awoke
on realisation of the Good

when he returned to the Father.
Blessed is he who restores
the sight of the spiritually blind!

The Holy Spirit chased them
with great haste, to wake them up!

Holding out his hand to those lying
helpless on the earth, he pulled up
those that were not yet awakened!
He told them how to know
their Father and His Son.

When they'd seen and heard Jesus,
he showed them how to savour
and feel him, the beloved one.

When Christ came teaching
about their Father, the unknowable,
inscrutable one, he breathed into
them meaning, action and will,
revealing the Light to very many.

Instantly they turned
inwards towards him.

The materialists were exiles
and failed to see his similitude,
and couldn't know him.

He came in bodily form
without obstacles,
for purity is unconquerable.

He again revealed new doctrine
about what's in our Father's heart,
having revealed His perfect Word!

When the Light had shone,
through his lips as well as his voice,
all Life was given new birth.
He passed on to them his
apperception of comprehension,
compassion and redemption.

Energy of spirit
flowed from our Father's
boundlessness and sublimity,
ending chastisement and torment,
for some had been led astray
from the light of His countenance.

Those in need of mercy had
fallen into falsehood and bondage.
He vanquished these foes
by his strength and enlightened
them with his teaching.

He became the Way for sheep
who had strayed from knowledge
into nescience.

He was a great find for seekers,
a foundation for those toppling,
flawlessness for those corrupted.

He was the good shepherd
who deserted the ninety-nine
that were safe and searched for
that one that had strayed.

He celebrated when he found
the lost sheep, for ninety-nine
is a number held in the left hand.

When one more is found,
one hundred is a number

held by the right.
It attracts what was
lacking in the left
and places it in the right.

One hundred signifies soundness;
it is our Father's number.

Even on the Sabbath day
he laboured for the sheep
fallen into the ditch.

He breathed new life into them
so they might know the Truth
inwardly and become sons
of inner knowledge.

What kind of Sabbath
is it that forbids salvation
to work so you may live?

From daylight above
which knows no night,
and from that sun which never
sets because it is flawless.

Utter from the heart
"I am the perfect day!
And in me dwells that light
which never sets."

Teach the Truth to those that
seek, and knowledge to those
fallen into the pit through falsehood.

Steady the stance of all who've
slipped and reach out with open arms
to all those who are sick at heart.

Feed the famished,
grant peace to the fatigued,
raise up all who wish to arise,
awaken all who wish to awaken!

For you are the
comprehension that has
been brought forward into light.

If power acts, it becomes
more powerful!

Pay attention to your own Real Self!
Don't spend time on that which
you've rejected from your petty self.

Don't return to the vomit
you've thrown up.
Don't be like moths or
worms that cause decay,
for you've already cast them out.
Don't make a home for Satan;
you've already vanquished that fiend!
Don't hold up those that form
barriers which have nearly fallen.

The lawless are the ones to scorch,
rather than the just.
The lawless work alone;
the righteous work amongst their flock.

Do the will of our Father;
we all come from Him!
Our Father is sublime;
His will is beneficent.
He has watched over you
so you may find peace.

He takes notice of your
works because His children
are His incense,
the grace of His Face.

Our Father loves His fragrance
and reveals it everywhere.

It combines with matter
and bestows perfume
on His light and peace;
He makes it superior
to shape and sound.

It's not the senses that smell
the perfume but the breath,
which attracts His fragrance
to itself and is subsumed.

He preserves and transfers
it back to its original home,
from where it first emerged,
the primary fragrance
that has grown cold.

It is a subtle form, like ice
which once was liquid,
but when breathed on, heats up.

Cold fragrance comes from duality,
so faith comes and dissolves division!

And brings forward the intense heat
of the Godhead that lives in Christ,
the Pleroma of Love.

So frigidity will never return,
and there'll be Oneness
and flawless thought.

This is the promise of the
Pleroma, for those who wait
for salvation from above.
While the hope
on which they are waiting
lies in the waiting.

For those whose similitude
is light without shadow,
the Pleroma is on its way.

The lack isn't because of the
boundlessness of our Father,
who allows time for the lack
to be healed.

Although no one says,
"The Flawless One
must come this way."

But the deepening of our
Father's Love is extensive
and the concept of falsehood
is nonexistent in Him.

It is faith which may fall
but can again stand up
in the knowing of Him,
and he who has been chosen
and who shall return;
this is metanoia.

So flawlessness breathed,
and chased away the sins of those
who'd fallen, to find repose.

Forgiveness is the light in
the lack, the Word of the Pleroma.

The doctor rushes to where
the disease is rampant
because it is his will.

He who bears a lack
does not conceal it
because someone possesses
what the other lacks.

So the Pleroma,
which is not lacking,
fills any lack in what it
provides for itself to fulfil.
So we might receive grace,
for when we lacked,
grace was deficient.

That causes our contraction
to smallness in a graceless place.

When this contraction was
received, He unveiled that which

was lacking, the Pleroma.
The finding of the Light of Truth,
which arose because it is constant.

This is why Jesus is referred
to as being "in their midst".
So those in perplexity might
receive a turning inwards,
and he might anoint them
with his precious salve.
The salve is our Father's
infinite compassion
and unconditional love,
which He hands to them.

Those whom He's anointed
have become flawless;
full jars receive ointment.
The jar empties of ointment
because there was a lack,
and the salve was applied.

His breath attracts healing,
by its own power;
for those without lack,

no seal need be broken
nor salve used.
What they lack our
flawless Father refills.

He is good;
He knows his plants,
because it is He who planted
them in His own garden.

Now His Eden
is a haven of peace.
This is the flawlessness
in the will of our Father
and these are the words
of His contemplation.

Each one of His words
comes from His will,
in the unveiling of His Word.

While they were at peace through
the depth of His meditation,
which was the First,
there issued a mind that spoke

the one Word of silent grace.
This was termed "thought",
for they were held in it
before it was unveiled.

It was the First,
when the will of Him
who willed, so willed it.

His will is what our Father
lives in, and is satisfied.
Nothing ever happens
without Him,
nor can anything happen
without His will,
which is inscrutable.

His mark is the will
that no one can know Him.

Nor is it possible to investigate
Him so as to know Him.

What He wills is "that",
even if it displeases those

in the way, seeking God,
desiring our Father.

For He knows all their
beginnings and their ends.
At their end He'll enquire
of them, directly.

The end is the final receipt of
knowledge about He who is
concealed and is our Father.
From whom the genesis issued
and to whom all shall return.

They have issued from the
splendour and rejoicing
of His Holy Name.

The name of our Father is the Son.
It is He who first named the One
who came from Him and is Himself.

He is that One to whom belongs
all that exists around Him,
and that is our Father.

His is the Name;
His is the Son;
He can be known.

The Name is unseen because
it is the enigma of the unseen,
which comes to ears that
are full of Him.

Our Father's name is unutterable,
but known through His Son.

The Name is Great.
Who will be capable
of uttering His holy Name?

Only our Father,
who owns the Name,
and his sons, in whom
the Name lives.

Since our Father is unborn,
He alone is the One who
created for Himself the Name,
before He created the Aeons,

so that His Name as Father
might rule as Lord.

That is His Name in Truth,
stable in control,
through His flawless force.

His Name is wordless.
Nor does His Name consist of
mere names; it is unseen.

He gave the Name to Himself alone,
for only He can know Himself
and has the power to give a Name.

For the nonexistent is nameless,
but the One who exists lives
with a name and He alone knows it.

The Father,
the Son,
is His Name!

He never concealed it in matter,
but it lived as for the Son;

He alone gives a Name.
The Name is Father,
for that Name is also the Son.

Where indeed would
Divine mercy find a Name
except in our Father?

A man will ask his neighbour,
"Who is it who can give a Name
to Him who existed before Himself?"
As if children never received
a name from their parents.

First we must pursue
the enquiry, "What does
the Name mean?"

It is the Name in Truth,
not the Name from our Father
but the Real Name!
He didn't receive the Name
on credit, as others might,
according to the way
that each name is given.

But this is the Real Name;
there's no one there to give it
to Him, for He's unnameable,
inscrutable, unknowable.

Until that time when He who
is flawless speaks of Him alone,
it is He who has authority
to utter the Name and know it.

When it pleased Him that
His Name, which is beloved,
should be His Son,
He named him "He who
came from the deep".

Christ spoke about concealed secrets,
knowing our Father is the Supreme
Being without wickedness.

So he brought himself to teach
about where He came from
and where He rests.
And to preach about the splendour
of the Pleroma, the magnitude of

his Father and His Divine sublimity.
About the place from where he came
and the realm where he was confirmed.

He'll be quick to return,
receiving manna and growth,
and his dwelling in the Pleroma.

All the rays from our Father are
Pleromas, and the source is the One
who created them in His own Self.
He designated their fate;
each is created so through their
own will they may return.

For where they place their will,
their source, He lifts them to the
great spiritual heights of their Father.

They rest their burden on
His head and they're maintained,
welcoming Him as if they'd
greeted His face with kisses.

Yet they don't always act this way
for they are not so exalted,
yet they are not deficient
in their Father's splendour.

They didn't regard their
Father as diminutive or severe,
or liable to anger, but knew
that He was without evil,
unshakeable and sublime,
knowing all space before
they originated and without
need to be taught.

This is the way of those who
already have some taste from
above of His boundless magnitude.

As they attend on the flawless One
who waits for them with open arms,
they won't descend to hell,
nor suffer envy, pain and death.

They will rest in peace, neither toiling
nor being twisted around the Truth.

For they are Truth; their Father is within,
they are in Him, who is flawless!
Undivided in His beneficence,
lacking nothing, at perfect peace,
rejuvenated in Spirit.

They'll be attentive to
finding their own source and
not endure loss to their soul.
This is the isle of the blessed,
this is their golden land.

The rest must understand
that it's inappropriate for me,
being in His place,
to speak about anything else.

It is from there that I come
to be and it is right to attend
all the time to our Father of All
and our real brothers,
those who benefit from
His unconditional love,

which is constantly poured out,
for He dwells in their midst.

They demonstrate in Truth
and dwell in Life Everlasting
and witness His Flawless Light
filled with their father's seed,
which lives in His heart and
the Pleroma, while His Holy Spirit
celebrates and magnifies
the One in whom He lives.

He is goodness;
His offspring are flawless,
fit to bear His Name.

He is our Father;
we are His children
whom He loves!

THE GREATEST
HUMAN EVIL IS
FORGETFULNESS OF
GOD

An early Gnostic text warning of the grave
spiritual dangers should the Soul lose hold of its essential
Self. It stresses the need for Recollection and Self
Remembering leading to eventual salvation.

FROM *Corpus Hermeticum VII*

Dear fellows, where are you
rushing to like drunkards, tipsy
and staggering on the rich wine
of reason, forgetful of God?

You cannot stomach it;
already you're about to vomit!

Halt! Sober up!

Elevate yourself by mental power.
Maybe not all of you can do that,
but some of you can!

For the degeneration that flows
from forgetfulness is drowning
the earth, infecting soul and body,
veiling the soul like a cloak and
stopping you from abiding in the heart.

So don't be swept away
by this mad flood!

Find the way into your heart!
Look for a good teacher
to show you the path
to the gates of remembrance.
Where there's a light,
radiant and bright,
free from darkness.

Where nobody is drunk,
but keeps their mental eye
on that Great Being who
wills to be known in their heart.

That Great Being cannot
be seen or heard, or spoken
or thought about,
only by a higher subtle
intellect that transcends
normal matters of the mind.

But first strip off the
soiled cloak you wear,
the foul mantle of forgetfulness,
the base of wickedness,
the link with evil,
the black pit,
the spiritual death,
the walking corpse,
the moving coffin,
the domestic rogue who
feeds on guile, which he relishes,
and conspires to cause your downfall.

Such is the habit;
the filthy coat you've put on,
that is your foe!

It suffocates you and drags you
down to its cruel self, into the gutter.

Otherwise, through aspiration
and seeing the beauty of Truth
and the Good that dwells in you,
you will come to despise this
vile enemy who plots to destroy you.

It ruins the mind and pollutes
the senses by muddying them
with gross materialism,
filling them with disgusting
lust for inane pleasure,
to prevent you from understanding
what you should understand!

And, what is worse,
it will stop you from seeing
forever what you should really see!

THE SECRET BOOK

ACCORDING TO

ST JOHN I, II & III

Introductory extracts from the "Apocryphon of John",
son of Zebedee, outlining Gnostic mythology. They see
Almighty God as the Source of all Being and describe the
structure of the Divine Cosmology before Genesis.
Probably composed around AD 180.

One day John,
brother of James,
a son of Zebedee,
was going to synagogue.

A Pharisee called Arimanios
met him and said,
"Where is your teacher,
the one you followed?"

John replied, "He's gone back
to the place he came from."

Arimanios said, "That
Nazarene has confused you.

He lied and closed your mind
and put you off the teachings
of our fathers!"

When I heard this
I left the synagogue
and went into the desert.

I was upset and said to myself,
"How was our Saviour chosen?
Why did he enter this world,
and who sent him?
And what is that place
that we'll all go to?"

While I was musing,
suddenly the heavens opened!
All creation glowed with light.

I was very frightened,
when I saw in the brilliant light
a boy, standing upright.

Then he changed into an old person,
then a young one, all in bright light,
so that there appeared, as it were,
three beings in one form.

Then this multiformed image
addressed me and said,
"John, why do you doubt?
Why are you terrified?
Are you a stranger to visions?

Don't be frightened.
It is I who am with you forever,
It is I who am the Father,
Mother and Son.

I am uncorrupted and pure.
I've come to enlighten you
on what exists, what is to come,
and what is to be.
So you may know about
the spiritual and the material realm,
the invisible and the visible,
and all about the Perfect Man.

Pay attention so you can
pass this on to others like you,
from the inheritance of this Perfect Man,
so they might know Truth.

This is my book on the
teachings of Jesus, my Messiah,
and the unveiling of God's mysteries,
which he taught, and his great
teachings secreted in silence."

I asked this triadic figure
if I might hear this Truth.

He proclaimed and answered:
"There is nothing that
can rule over the One.

It is that One which is God
and Father of the All.

The transcendent, immanent,
deathless Self, shining as pure light,
which nobody can see.

This absolute spirit is
more than a God,
for nothing is above Him
and all is in Him.
He rests alone
and is independent.
He is perfect; He needs nothing
and lacks for nothing.

He is boundless,
unsearchable,
immeasurable,
invisible.

External,
internal,
eternal,
ineffable,
unnameable.

He is flawless,
impeccable,
incorporeal;
neither great
nor small.

He has no quantity,
quality or attributes.
He is inscrutable
and beyond time.

He is King of Kings,
bestowing life,
knowledge, goodness,
mercy and salvation.

He is at rest, in silence,
as primordial Being
and pure Light.

He looks at himself
alone in perfect peace,
the fount of living waters
exercising divine will.

This complete totality,
the Aeon above Aeons,
the power and glory,
the virgin spirit,
the womb for creation,
Mother-father,

archetypal Man,
macrocosm and microcosm.

He gazed at the Whole,
in the pure light of
Absolute Consciousness,
and conceived its sole offspring,
a luminous spark.

He was granted a cooperative spirit,
which was clairvoyant intellect.

That spirit rested with
the anointed one, the Christ,
and wished to create by the Word,
from its Will.

By the grace of the spirit,
out of the light of the anointed,
all powers originated.

Beauty, as the first angel, Harmozel,
and with this eternal realm,
loveliness, truth and form.

Oroiael is the second,
angelic light, reflection,
cognisance and memory,

Daueithal was third,
intelligence, love
and archetypal ideal form.

Eleleth was fourth,
perfection, peace and wisdom.

From his will the first
manifestation was named:
the Primordial Man, the Adam.

His son Seth was placed
in the second realm,
with the souls of Saints.

In the fourth realm were
placed unrepentant souls,
unacquainted
with the Perfection.

They later repented and
inhabited the fourth light,
to glorify the invisible spirit.

Wisdom conceived an idea
derived from herself,
to show an image.

But her consort did not agree,
so she conceived alone.

Her birth was imperfect
for it lacked her consort's will
and had a misshapen form;
it was named Ialtabaoth.

It was snake-like,
with a leonine face,
and from its eyes
flashed lightning.

She cast it out so none of
the immortals might know it,
and enveloped it in a glowing cloud.

She put a throne in the middle
of the cloud so it would be invisible,
except to the Mother Of All Living.

Then the Primal Creator, Almighty God,
ordered all things in Perfection."*

*The two final verses commence a new
development of ideas and are omitted.

THUNDER

Aunique Gnostic revelation by a mysterious
Female Deity, stressing the importance of the essential
"I Am-ness". Also known as the "Perfect Mind", it contains
parallels with ancient Indian literature which refers to
the I AM form.

I have issued from a Great Power
and visit all who contemplate me;
I have been discovered
by those who search diligently.

Pay attention, those that meditate
upon me, and listen well!
All of you who are patiently waiting,
take me to your Self!

Don't dismiss me from your mind
and don't let your inner voices
despise me; don't forget me at any
time or place; be watchful!

I am the first and the last,
I am both respected and ignored,
I am both harlot and holy.

I am wife and virgin,
mother and daughter,
organs of my mother,
barren, yet many are my sons.

I am She whose marriage
is auspicious, but I am husbandless.

I am the midwife who doesn't
carry the balm of birth pains.
I am bride and groom
sired by my spouse;
I am mother of my father,
sister of my husband,
and he's my son.

I am slave of He who anointed me.
I am ruler of my children, but
He is the One from whom I was born.
He shall be my Son in time;
my strength is from Him!

I am the rod of His potency
in His youthful virility,
and He is the staff of my old age.
Whatever He wills, happens.

I am the unfathomable silence
and the thought that comes often,
the voice of many sounds,
and the word that appears frequently.

I am the meaning of my Name.
Why am I despised?
Do you love me and hate
those who love me too?

If you deny me then admit me,
You, who pretend to tell the truth
about me, really lie.

Yet you who've lied about me
also tell the Truth.
If you know me, forget me,
and those who don't know me,
let them know!

I am knowledge and ignorance.
I am embarrassment and effrontery,
shameless and ashamed.
I am courage and fright.

I am war and peace. Listen!
I am disgraced yet almighty.

Notice my poverty and richness.
Don't be unkind to me when I'm
thrown out upon the ground.

You'll find me hidden in those
yet to come; don't peer at me
when I'm on the dung heap.

Don't desert me or cast me out;
you'll find me in the Kingdom.

Don't gaze at me when I'm ejected
in disgrace, nor mock me.

Don't hurl me amongst those
who are slain violently.
I am merciful and cruel.

Be vigilant!
Don't despise my servitude.
Don't admire my self-control;
don't forsake me in my ineptitude.

Never fear my power;
don't hate my timidity
or pour scorn on my arrogance.

I am She who dwells in all terror,
the strength and the trembling.

I am She who is pathetic and
pleased in a pleasant place.
I am stupid and I am wise.

Why do you despise me
in your councils?
I'll be quiet among the quiet.

I shall manifest and speak,
yet why do Greeks hate me?
I am a Philistine among Philistines,
yet have the wisdom of Athens
and craftiness of the barbarians.

My image is great in ancient Egypt,
but is nothing amongst Philistines.

I've been hated everywhere,
but also adored.
I am that which people call
life and you call death.

I am called the Law
and lawlessness.
I am the hunted
and the captured.

I am the dispersed
and the collected.
I don't keep festivals,
but have many feasts.

I am both godless and
She who knows God is Great!
I am the One you've
contemplated and mocked.

I am ignorant, yet I teach.
I am despised, yet admired.

I am the One who conceals
and then reveals her Self.

But when you conceal
your Self, I shall appear.

When you appear I'll hide.
Hold me to your Self
from comprehension and regret.

Take me to your Self
in ugly and ruined places.
Rob those who are good,
even in their ugliness.

Ashamed, take me to
your Self shamelessly;
scold my organs in yourself.

Advance, all that know
me and my organs;
establish high creatures
amongst the lowly.

March onto childhood;
don't hate that state
because it appears tiny.
Don't reject greatness
in smallness.

My nature is peace,
but war comes from me.

I am an exile
and a subject;
I am substance
and unsubstantial.

Those who do not cling
to me are ignoramuses,
but those who dwell in
my substance know me.

Those who are close
don't know me.
When you are near,
I'm distant.

On the day you're distant,
I am close.
I am within, in your heart;
I am your true nature,
the creativity of your Self.